Scottish Borders Library Service

3 41

D1179083

GOOD NEIGHBOURS

Some Recollections of an English Village and its People, written down by

WALTER ROSE

ISIS
LARGE PRINT
Oxford and Orlando

Copyright © Cambridge University Press

First published in Great Britain 1942
by Cambridge University Press

Published in Large Print 1999 by ISIS Publishing Ltd,
7 Centremcad, Osney Mead, Oxford OX2 0ES, and
ISIS Publishing, PO Box 195758,
Winter Springs, Florida 32719-5758, USA
by arrangement with Cambridge University Press

All rights reserved

The moral right of the author has been asserted

British Library Cataloguing in Publication Data
Rose, Walter, b. 1871
    Good neighbours : some recollections of an English village
    and its people. – Large print ed.
    1. Large type books 2. Haddenham (England) – Social life and
    customs
    I. Title
    942.5'93

ISBN 0753150921

SCOTTISH BORDERS LIBRARY SERVICE

ACCESSION No.	CLASS No.
481294	

Printed and bound by MPG Books Ltd, Bodmin, Cornwall

Contents

Dedicated to all who love
the old English village

Preface

SCOTTISH
BORDERS
LIBRARY
SERVICE

A man who knows the history of his village has also a sense of responsibility; he realizes that his unique information ought to be shared with other people, and he feels obliged to place it on permanent record.

This sense of duty is deepened by the awareness that conditions of life are still changing, with a rapidity that our fathers never dreamed of, so that those born into life as it is today cannot be expected to understand the manner of life lived by their grandparents.

These reasons prompt me to attempt to describe the village as it was at the time of my boyhood; the village that some forty years before my birth had passed through the throes of its enclosure, and since then had settled itself into the stable life of farmer, labourer, and artisan.

Enriched by experience and mature consideration, I find that the village of my boyhood has now a character that, naturally, I did not then appreciate. It is now possible to review it in the light of its preceding influences, the centuries of open-field cultivation of the soil that preceded the enclosure of 1830. Much that I know of the character and dispositions of its natives I now attribute to the centuries of preceding life throughout which the village extended its habitations and the cultivation of the three-thousand-odd acres of good soil that forms its parish.

This assumption gives clues to what is otherwise hard to explain. It is possible to see that the excess of population, with consequent poverty, at the close of the eighteenth century, was due to the fact that the extension of soil cultivation had reached the limit of the parish. The old system had answered well for long but had served its purpose; there was need for a more intensive system of cultivation, which resulted in the enclosure and redistribution of the land.

Without remarks for or against, it is apparent that, to the natives, the process must have been like the uprooting of old trees. What had taken a thousand years to establish could not be destroyed in a single year. Although the subsequent life appeared placid, I am now aware of the underlying spirit that lived on: the hankering of the rural heart for the soil of which it had been dispossessed.

The spirit of independence — and this may be of some interest to historians — has always been a characteristic of the natives. It is of moment to note that, throughout the centuries of pre-enclosure life, this village rarely had a residential overlord to order its habits and ways. Its principal manor was vested in a far-distant monastery, and was ruled through agents at the manorial farm. Evidence remains that these rules were enforced and services duly rendered; beyond which the mind is free to picture the holders each secure on his plot, or plots, of land, and to understand that an assured independence naturally developed from this systematic cultivation.

Some authorities assert that life under the manorial system was hard; whether it was so or not in general, in this particular instance we have proof of prosperity. The fact that, in the year 1625, the copyholders, making a united effort to rid themselves of services on the manorial lands, paid over for release the sum of £1562, is some revelation of their thriving condition. Further proof is found in documents, under dates 1644-5-6, which reveal levies for money, live and dead stock, and services, made for the support of the Parliamentary troops, to the sum of £1744.

The remembrance of the early villagers was long; their traditions were handed down the centuries from father to son. Prior to the enclosure no radical change of village life had taken place. The sons had inherited and cultivated the separate acres of their fathers, in due time to hand them on to their own children. The system had taken centuries to create and seemed likely to continue for all time; it was destined to end with the enclosure.

The village of my boyhood may be regarded as the result, with a life somewhat mangled by the operations of its birth, yet in which some semblance of its parentage remained.

The subsequent half-century has witnessed a radical change: as a result of the introduction of machinery in agriculture, and of general mass production — methods made necessary by the advance in wages — the land no longer supports its people. The labour formerly expended on the soil has drifted away to other occupations; the youth who, in the old days, would have taken his place on a farm, now cycles to work in a nearby town; the labourer clad in corduroy is a rarity. Not less significant of entire change is the simple fact that "hunger for the land" has ceased in the hearts of the workers.

Still greater is the change of life resulting from the inflow of residents from towns, many of whom have bought the ancient cottages, and, by judicious restorations, have made them into charming homes. Strange to write, yet none the less true, it is mainly to these folk that the natives are indebted for a right appreciation of the character of the village. Equally true is the fact that the cottagers are more comfortably housed in the new houses erected by the district authorities. The village is passing through another period of transition; influences, never known before in its long history, are reforming its life and character as it is destined to be.

That destiny is, of course, impossible to foretell, though I think the indications are that its general character is indestructible. Smooth roads, new paths, with here and there an angle improved, do not eradicate the haphazard irregularity of its ways. A water system may cause its wells to be filled up, yet drainage will but purify its central stream. The eye is soon accustomed to overhead wires and the poles for electric light and telephone; the brilliance of the passing express enhances the stable quietude that prevails.

Happily, the temperament which now avails itself of every improvement as it comes to hand, is, at the same time, insistent on preserving as far as possible all that is of value belonging to the past. The old homes, improved and beautified, look benevolently on the modern bus and cars as they speed by. It seems to be a happy relinking of the present with the past; an appreciation of the virtues that belong to each; an acknowledgement that only by so doing can life to-day be truly beautiful.

I desire to acknowledge with gratitude the encouragement and help received from Frank Kendon in preparing and revising the manuscript for press.

W. R

June, 1942

CHAPTER
ONE

The Village

I am inclined to regard the year 1871 as a fortunate date for my birth; it was early enough for me to catch the fag end of the old order of life that, even then, was rapidly passing: and late enough for me to witness the change over to conditions still continuing to-day. Hence I can claim to belong to both old and new; and, whereas little purpose would be served in describing what everyone to-day can see for themselves, the life of my early years has already become interesting and strange.

To have lived in the same village for almost the whole of one's life is rare enough to-day. To be of a succession of fathers, of whom all lived in the same place, is even more rare. It makes me feel that I *belong* to the village and the village to me. *They* had no desire to move away; it was always good enough for them, as I, also, have found it to be for myself. The spirit of its life flowed in their veins, as it continues to flow in mine. They all lie within the embrace of its soil, as I hope, in due course, myself to lie.

To these, my revered fathers, I owe a great debt, for they passed on to me much village lore. They are all gone, and I am quite unable to repay them, save by

1

passing on to others what they passed on to me. It was at their knees that I learned of the ways and doings of former years; especially of the different order of life before the enclosure of the fields. It was in the old homes, at the firesides and amid survivals of their older world that they told me their stories of past days. It always seemed to give them pleasure to tell; it was delight to me to listen and learn. I am confident that nothing would have gratified them more than to know that eventually some of those stories would be put into print.

To look at the life of my boyhood, now, is like looking at an existence so different in character as to seem almost foreign. Yet changes came so quietly and naturally that, save for the later, tragic experience of the 1914–18 war, we scarcely knew that life was changing. We were always busy, and if new conditions at length forced themselves upon our notice, even then the heart and mind inclined to a vague belief that matters would mend again and the old order return.

It goes without saying that the village adopted each improvement as it came along. It is true that many of them have made life easier. It was at the point of this pen to add "happier", but I am not quite so sure of that. On looking back, I am conscious of a serenity that does not seem to exist to-day; an ability to see delight in natural surroundings that is not so evident now.

These old people, like their fathers before them, lived in direct contact with the soil. Its influence was born into them; they had never been separated from its teachings. Of education, as it is understood to-day, they had little or none; they learned the deep-rooted secrets of nature, knowledge worthy enough, it seems, to colour their lives with simple joy.

The land to which their eyes were turned was regarded as the great benefactor. It craved their study, their thoughts, and efforts, and in return yielded them their food and health. It was a deep and enduring sentiment, an attachment that had continued down the years from the time when the soil had first been reclaimed from the primeval forest. As this land had always sufficed for the needs of their fathers, so none expected or desired but that it would continue to serve theirs also. Their wish was to remain on the land; the labourer's highest ambition was to have a plot to cultivate on his own.

The village was but little affected by a railway three miles away, which had been built about nine years before my birth and was still a novelty. When my father took me for my first ride on it, he promised that I would be able to look into the tops of the chimneys of houses that we passed. Older men remembered, and often spoke of, the first cutting of even more distant canals, which had formerly served the needs of the district. To visit either railway or canal was a rare delight. I always associated the railway with the smell of creosote, a good smell, to my notion, and an exciting change from the undiluted air of the village.

Supplies were fetched into the village by horse-dray. Groceries, coal, my father's deals, and all materials were hauled from the station by road. The farmers sent away corn, hay, and straw by train; and this, so old men declared, was slowly impoverishing the land. The

3

making of that railway, they said, was the worst event that had ever happened to the district; because the goodness of the soil was being taken away, and nothing put in its place. To them it was a policy that would lead to disaster.

Changes were at work indeed; yet they were only driblets of an outside influence, too weak as yet to have much effect upon the established tenor of village life. I was out of my teens before the first telephone wires penetrated into its history. A telegram was received with ominous forebodings (indeed, I still feel them). There was 1s. 6d. to pay before you opened it — for having it brought from the nearest town — and it was not likely to be sent except for most urgent reasons, usually illness or the death of a relative.

The village was a cluster of ancient homesteads, formerly the habitations of yeomen who had farmed the scattered acres of the parish. It was about a mile long, a straggle of houses and out-buildings without plan, alongside a small stream that had supplied its original settlers with water. Those homesteads, by their size and capacity, showed the evolution of the ancient community. Some were much larger than others, and had ample yards with barns of several bays, sheds for cattle, and a pightle of pasture attached. These had been the homesteads of elder sons who had inherited their fathers' lands. The smaller houses, which were often comfortable thatched cottages, had been the homes of younger sons who had inherited what was left of the estate, and had taken up, cleaned and cultivated fresh acres from the surrounding belt of forest, so as to secure their position in the village. Most of the more ancient homes had buildings of some sort attached; cottages that had none were of a later date. The whole irregular group told the unwritten story of a developing community, a group of pastoral folk, holding their lands under the ancient system of manorial tenure, a village that had continued to grow as long as a narrowing belt of forest remained from which acres could be taken for tillage by those who had no land.

The process went on until the whole three-thousand-odd acres that comprised the parish were taken up into cultivation. It followed then that those who could not get land of their own must needs work for others; and so eventually the system of permanent wage employment began. To the employer it was more convenient than the occasional hire of those who also had their own plots to till. For those landless labourers the cottages without buildings were built. They paid weekly rents.

This was the order of village life before the Enclosure, and it illustrates the type of village into which I was born. The reclamation of fresh land had reached the boundary; the expansion of pastoral life and livelihood had found its limit; the problem of an increasing population had been acute. It was evident that the system that had served many generations had failed to meet the existing need. Besides, for one holder to cultivate separate acres in different parts of the parish was obviously wasteful and did not encourage improved methods of agriculture. Operations on a larger scale were beginning to take the place of individual efforts; as in craft work the drift was towards mass production; and it was clear that land in large blocks would give a larger yield — a need made more imperative by war.

To give effect to these changes, Parliament passed separate Acts for redistributing and enclosing the land of parishes. It was not a mere enclosing of waste commons; it was the compulsory enclosing of all land held in common by the people. Yet, although they were not blind to the advantages of enclosed land in one block, most of the holders dreaded a forced enclosure. They knew full well that it was by no means a simple rearrangement of land, under which each holder would retain the same acreage in one block instead of in several. By the experiences of other parishes, already enclosed, they had learned what to expect. Commissioners, empowered by law, would arrive, and for the time being, all the land would be vested in them. The surveying and the new allocation of land would of necessity take time, during which no one would know which land to cultivate — the experience of the village was that a season's arable crop was lost. They knew, too, that the commissioners' fees, together with the cost of remaking the public roads, the planting of hedges, digging of ditches, and the erection of fences to protect the young growing quicks around the newly arranged fields, would all be chargeable on the land — not, as it is now, a debt spread over a period for payment, but to be paid forthwith. Also, instead of the Church tithe being collected in kind — as the tenth shock of corn, cock of hay, bucket of milk, lamb, calf, or newly born pig — a block of land would be appropriated as the permanent property of the Church.

To the holders of one or two acres only, the enclosure offered no advantage; yet they were obliged to fall into line with the holders of many acres, and were subject to the same proportion of expense. Such men were poor; and if they were receiving parish relief, the land allotted to them after enclosure was entered in the award as the property of the parish officers. Others had small mortgages secured on their plots; these were suddenly faced with the need of money to pay for redemption and to meet the enclosure expenses. Unable to raise the money, many parted with their ancestral plots for what they could get.

Though I live on the same soil, and remember vividly the stories told by several who passed through this experience, I still find it difficult to conceive the revolution of village life that resulted. The yeoman no longer existed; in his place the farmer was established. The small cultivator of one or two acres, who had also worked for others in his spare time, now became a labourer working for a weekly wage. Those yeomen who held many acres, yet had not the spare capital with which to meet the expenses, had their acreage reduced accordingly. My great-grandfather's holding was reduced from 97 acres, with rights of grazing, to 40, yet many held that he came out of the ordeal fairly well. The operation threw a quantity of land on the market, much of which was bought by a capitalist, a stranger to the village, who was said to have come from the north of England. My own people left the land and turned instead to the building crafts; but my grandfather always used to regard this change as a mistake.

The village as I knew it, in the days of my youth, still showed the effects of these experiences; the philosophy of its life had been changed but not remoulded by the settlement of the enclosure. The forty years since that event were to many natives but as a day, their hearts still clung to the semi-free life when, without fear of trespass, all were able to ramble from end to end of the long parish, along the lanes and over the baulks that separated the multitude of separate acres. They could not forget the soil, once their own, and now for ever forfeited, the loss of which constituted their humiliation. Some, when boys, had run the tracks through the long mowing grass, when, in ceremonial form, the yeomen had assembled, each with scythe, to cut the meads that lined the brooks on each side of the parish. Others had helped to tend the common herd that left the village daily to graze the portion of the parish left fallow, or the meads after the hay was carried. The love of the soil bred by that kind of life was not accidental, but an inborn spirit, a sentimental trust bequeathed by many ancestors who had lived in a like way.

That love did not die, even though after the enclosure the majority of the villagers had no rood of land to call their own, nor even to cultivate by rental. In penury they tilled the land of others, yet it continued to animate them with its subtle spirit; its lore still found expression through their lives.

As carpenters to the village we had special opportunities to know and observe our neighbours. Our place, halfway up the tree of social status, put us into touch with farmers at the top and labourers at the bottom. We kept their farmhouses and cottages in good repair, and when they had done with them at last, we sent them to their rest in good coffins. On the whole, our intercourse was happy: they accepted us as integral to the village life, as we knew ourselves to be.

No farm or cottage could carry on for long without our services. When we repaired a threshing floor or the mewstead of the barn we could not do so without knowing what they were for. It was important to know the ways and needs of the milkers while putting up new stalls for the cows. The millers, too, were always in need of our help. We repaired the mills, both wind-driven and waterdriven, and knew every secret of their construction and exactly how they worked. Certainly there was no lack of interest and variety in our craft; it was ever a healthy, honest service to our fellow men, and one that was appreciated. The poor were glad to have their cottage homes made comfortable, and we saw, as we worked, their scanty means. We learned to appreciate the simple beauty often allied with poverty, and the dignity of character to be found at times among unfruitful surroundings.

The structural work of the village had its special fascination — its appeal to the craft spirit. We continually handled the work of bygone craftsmen, workers of greater or less ability, known creators, whose enduring handiwork was their only monument. We knew them to be of the past, workers of the village in its earlier history; they had their own particular methods, expressive of life at the time when the work was done. Elm was a wood they largely used, no doubt because it was (and still is) native and plentiful. Elm abounded in the beams of the houses and barns and all other buildings. The ruling need, of course, had been utility; but now and then we came across evidence of the craftsman's natural urge to beauty — in the design, or in ornament by carving or in mouldings.

If such work sometimes seemed rough, it had now been softened by kindness of time; the touch of thousands of hands had added to its subtle charm. Or, out of doors, nature had herself adorned their work with abundant lichens of many colours; even the weather-boards of the old barns were covered over with these delicate and lovely encrustations.

Every piece of work out of the past that came under our notice had its own special teaching. It told of days when a craftsman's tools were rougher and fewer than those with which we went to work; and it always bore witness to the constant triumph of craftsmanship, the skill of hands surmounting difficulties. The beam that had been shaped by the adze alone, before planes were generally used, had its own special charm; each disk-mark left by the blade expressed a separate act of the worker. It was as though we could see him at his work, with the log lying there at his feet; we felt and shared his conscientious care, his concern to keep the line of work straight and the finish clean. Yes, and we had to admit that his ability exceeded our own; we could not handle the adze with half his skill: the improvement of tools had lowered the need for personal ability.

If the village had been a growing place with continual need for new houses and new roads, our work would not have been so much associated with past days. As it was, through our repairs of the old, the past and present life were interlinked in our experience until we became familiar with both. We experienced the changes that were at work; many threshing barns no longer served their original purposes, and some were falling into decay. Even such an invention as the separator was not without its effect on us as carpenters: we were no longer called in to make those large shallow cases of wood, which, lined with lead by the plumber, were used as flats for the old-fashioned farm dairy. It was once my lot (but only once) to make a "dolly" (a stirrer) for the washing copper. Dolly-making could he done almost wholly on the lathe; but to make a "betty", its companion-help, used for straining the washed clothes over the copper, one needed the tools and all the skill of a joiner.

Galvanized sheet iron for covering roofs first appeared when I was a boy, and I remember my father's interest in it as a cheap and effective covering. But we did not foresee how widely it would come to be used, nor how much its use would mar the countryside. The picturesque roofs of thatch were becoming less and less lasting; the straw, damaged by the threshing machine, would not stand the weather so long; and the thatchers' charges were going up at the same time. This, together with the dread of fire and the fact that insurance rates were double, had made thatch unpopular; yet nothing since contrived to take its place can compare with it for comfort.

Canal-building had brought us slates from Wales. The church (unfortunately) and a cottage, not now standing, were the first to be covered with them. For years slates were to be regarded as the ideal covering, an opinion that, happily, is no longer held. When the G.W.R. was made, large tiles from Bridgwater in Somerset came along, and many barns were covered with these. They were never quite satisfactory; snow filtered between them, and the old roofs were so steep that the tiles were too easily dislodged by winds and used to slide to the ground. Galvanized iron had none of these disadvantages; yet its use was an irritation to the true craftsman. Our hands were accustomed to the responsive feel of wood; we did not like handling the harshness of galvanized iron, or the look of it afterwards. One of father's men would say: "Even a wheelbarrow would catch cold under it."

We ourselves, alas, were responsible for some spoliation. Even if it were possible, it would now be sad for me to say how many beautiful old leaded windows we pulled out of cottage windows, inserting large panes of glass in their places. The cottagers did not like the small diamond-shaped or oblong panes; they were often of very old glass, mottled, and with undulating surfaces that reflected glancing lights and shadows; but it was hard work to keep them clean; and when they were clean what was seen through them was often distorted. Crude methods of glass-making had left imprisoned sparklets in them, small eyes that radiated tiny revolving lights. In some, a chemical action had taken place where glass and lead came into contact, and an iridescent film of colour — as of violet, mingled with gold — had spread, with graduated strength, over the glass. This, however, was the development of years of neglect, and did not happen where the cleaning rag had been active.

New glass was cheap and we could cut it to any size; it was clear and free from eyes, and all declared how much better it was. Within the windows, so transformed, the cottagers stood their geraniums and other flowers in pots and viewed them with pride through the large new panes of glass. Not until the old glass had become rare and almost unobtainable was its particular beauty appreciated and its value known.

It speaks well for the spirit of the village that, in spite of all that has been lost, destroyed, or taken away, its world-old character remains. Up till now it has not been possible to remove its cottages and homes, yet they, in their turn, are now threatened by modern danger. The sanitary inspector distrusts them, and is horrified when they do not exactly conform with present-day by-laws. Their floors and walls are uneven; their ceilings are not high enough; their stairways are often winding and dangerous, and their windows too small for the regulation light and air. Still worse, they were built long before damp-courses were thought of. Over their old, warm, embracing thatch the cold official sword waits the word to fall.

Certainly, nothing should stand in the way of health, and health depends, no doubt, on the condition of our homes. Yet we may run into danger if we forget that mind is a controlling power of health, and that all that makes for greater interest in life influences the body for good at the same time. Sentiment — often despised — is, after all, one of the strongest of forces for good or evil; and the mind able to enjoy its daily bread of beauty is more likely to be associated with a healthy body than the mind starved of beauty. No one of reflective mind can possibly separate the old-world cottage from the lives once lived in it by those, now gone, to whom we owe so much. Its going is like the severance from a friend, a departure that takes with it one more joy of life.

CHAPTER
TWO

The Farm

Of course many of the yeomen's homesteads continued to serve their agricultural purposes after the enclosure; but others were newly built on blocks of land away from the village, and at once one feature of the original life was broken — the unity of its homesteads, almost all of which were formerly clustered in the village itself.

By the time of my birth those old homesteads had been enlarged to cope with the extra land that had been added to each Their appearance suggested thrift and prosperity, their life stability, a settled course that moved with the regularity of the seasons.

The greater part of the parish was under arable cultivation; there had been prosperous times during which good profits had been made from corn. Labour at low rates had been plentiful, and still was so. One heard of land that had been cleaned to the last degree of perfection; so that men searching in vain for twitch on the ploughed land, had taken some from the hedgerow bank in order to have something to show the farmer when he made his round of inspection; also of the hoeing of wheat crops twice, or thrice, as the need was and labour availed. The labourers were never slow to express their own ideas on farm management. Old men told of the old laborious ways with favour, and praised them to the discredit of the hastier, cheaper methods that came in when foreign corn brought down the price of the home supply. They also deplored the laying down of land to grass that followed; it would, they said, reduce the demand for labour.

The village was still maintained by its land; its wealth filtered through the farmers' hands to the labourers and others who formed the community. Thus the soil, as before enclosure, was still the ruling influence, and the farmers, because they were farmers, exercised a control to which all others, more or less, conformed.

Edge farm had its regular labourers; men (some of whom had worked on the place since boyhood) who never thought of changing their places of employment, and boys and youths starting in on the same life-long career. They were a sedate sort of humanity, patient and uncomplaining. It could be said quite truly that their lives had few amenities; yet nature (so it seems) had granted them some compensations. It may be that their contentment was due to health and the outdoor life, with appetites that made simple fare a feast. They had a native sense of humour, an ability to see the funny side of misfortune that is not usual with an ailing body.

Education had not been compulsory, and the cottager was so needy that formerly parents were obliged to send the boy of nine years to work on the land. The result was that many men could neither read or write. My father said that at church or chapel it had been usual to read out the hymns two lines at a time, for only about one in twelve could read.

The working clothes were corduroys, subdued by long use to the colour of the earth, though rarely they were washed to a creamy whiteness that seemed unnatural. The men's trousers were strapped, or tied with string, under the knees; this, they said, kept in the warmth above and also gave freedom to kneel, or stoop, at work. For work during dirty weather, or for hedging and ditching and such-like rough tasks, long leathern gaiters, buttoned from the ankle to the hips, were worn.

They wore hard, heavy boots, the clean weight of them often doubled by the soil that clung to them while following the plough, so that each step taken over the furrows demanded a sustained upward pull; the ploughman and the boy who led the horses were known by their manner of walking — a to-and-fro, sideways sway of the head and shoulders down to the pit of the stomach — a gait of which they could not rid themselves even when walking on hard roads.

To work and back again, the tread of those labourers rarely quickened; their heavy boots pounded the earth with regular step. The alert townsman, used to light boots and quick steps over smooth pavements, thought them slow. But disillusionment came when the novice attempted to keep pace with them at harvest or hay work. Then, with chagrin, he learned the truth about their amazing speed and endurance.

They had native knowledge of everything about the farm or fields; they knew the ways and habits of horses, cattle, sheep, and pigs; between them and their work there went an intuitive sense of unison, inarticulate, yet understood by both man and animal, and these abilities were inherited rather than taught, and made proficient by lifelong experience.

It was right that to them life should move at its regular pace. (Let the man who would hurry try the game over a ploughed field, with a clod of earth hanging to each boot.) The cattle did not understand speed; their lives were ordered by the passing of the seasons, their movements attuned to the growth of herbage. Only the well-timed process of nature would increase their size and put flesh on their bones. This the farmer and his men understood, for the principle regulated their lives; their manner of speech was slow — what they had to say about the weather and prospect of crops was said with deliberate gravity; and the more rural the environment the graver and slower they were. There was no shortage of labour and so the year was always long enough for all this work that had to be done. Everything on the well-managed farm had its time. No effort of theirs could advance the day for the hay or corn harvest, or bring roots to maturity before their proper month. The regularity of life came of conforming to nature's laws; it was a system that appeared destined to continue for all time — a life separate and secure, always immune from the eager troubles that worried tradesfolk.

Labour on the soil was subject to the soil; no Higher Authority then dictated the terms and conditions of employment. The land from which the farmer drew his wealth was at his service, and rewarded him strictly according to his ability as a farmer. This gave him an enviable independence; all others were more or less subject to human authority, but nature alone was his monitor. A few became autocratic and aped the manner of squires; but most of them retained the simple ways of their yeomen ancestors.

Each farm was an establishment separate to itself, with an order of life largely independent of any other. Near the dwelling-house, but separated from it by a dwarf stone wall and a cobble path, would be a large yard, in which lay manure in various stages of decomposition. The manure had a comfortable smell, hinting of rich soil and good husbandry. Near the pigsties perhaps it was at times overpowering; near the stables it was often harsh with ammonia; but by the heap from the cowhouse the air was always mellow and suggested sweet hay and meadow grass. The whole, mingled together, formed a sombre mass, almost dry on the surface, yet treacherous to walk on. Unseen quagmires and pools of dark juicy liquid often lurked beneath, which it was wisdom not to disturb.

Close by stood the large threshing barn, its large doors opening generously on the farmyard. Through those doors came the clean straw from the threshers; for in there the corn was formerly threshed by flail for the livestock — oats, peas and beans for the horses and sheep, barley for the beer that all on the farm drank, and wheat also for their bread. All of this that could be spared from home consumption was taken to the market for sale. Sacks filled with corn and carefully tied, leaned against the mewstead. Each sack had the name of the farmer and farm stencilled on its side.

19

To step from the manure yard into the barn was to pass from muck to cleanliness. It was the parlour of the farm, where dirt was not allowable. The planks of its threshing floor were smooth with use; the timbers of its walls and roof soared aloft in venerable regularity; they still exhaled the scent of wood, the centuries-old fragrance drawn from some long-forgotten forest where they were felled. The deeps of its bays were obscure in semi-darkness, except where a shaft of light like an arrow pierced a crevice in its old boarded wall. The wealth of the fields was stored there after each harvest; bays filled with ripe corn, the result of twelve months' planning and labour; sheaves upon sheaves, all neatly tied and stacked, a compact bulk of provender for man and beast, all secure beneath the thatch, awaiting the flail.

The men who used those flails worked in couples. Standing face to face, with sheaves of corn between, they made their swinging blows alternately and with precision, as blacksmiths do when beating iron on the anvil. They often worked in list slippers, to avoid crushing the corn; and as the work was clean they had not the rough appearance that was usual to carters and stockmen. The threshing lasted through the winter, and they therefore escaped the discomforts of the open fields at that season. When the harvest was good and the barn was not large enough to take all the corn grown, ricks outside were built, resting on stone stattles that had mushroom-shaped tops to puzzle and prevent the mice.

Opposite the barn, on the other side of the farmyard, was the stable, where heavy horses with large hairy legs ranged side by side. It had its own peculiar atmosphere, the smell of rich, compressed old hay cut from the stack outside; manure, urine and the breath of horses, mingled with the dank exudations from a century of similar use. The stable was the citadel of the carters or ploughmen — by which dual title they were known — and the boys who helped them.

In comparison with the threshers they were a rougher and hardier race. Their work lay outdoors in almost all kinds of weather; their garments were like the soil in colour, and of a substance that would keep the rain from the skin. Their job was to keep the horses in condition, a team to each man. Each had his separate locked bin in which the weekly allowance of corn was stored. He carried the key on his person, or hid it secretly, to stop his fellow carters from helping themselves. Each was out to get as much corn as possible for his own team; to fetch more corn from the granary when the farmer was away was not looked upon as theft. And the farmer, knowing this, was careful to keep the door padlocked; yet the men had methods of forcing the staple and tapping it back into place again, just tight enough to hold and to be drawn when the chance offered.

The carter's zeal for his horses' welfare might rightly excuse any failings that accompanied the virtue. To have one's horses ripe in form, alert, with shining coats and fat rumps, was a brave advertisement of the stability of the farm. The head carter was granted the pick of the teams; his pride was to harness them in the best wagon, with its wheels painted vermilion, its body yellow, and the name of farmer and farm emblazoned on the front board.

No suburban "gent" was more particular about appearance than the carter of his horses. The brass harness of the collars shone with polishing; a belt, adorned with equally bright ornaments, passed between the forelegs, joining the collar to the belly-band. The leather was all dark and flexible, each buckle was fastened with care to give the horses freedom of movement, together with maximum of power. The horses themselves seemed to be conscious of the honour of being in the wagon, and to know that new experiences awaited them on the roads away from the farm.

The farmer was equally proud of them and equally anxious to maintain their reputation. With satisfaction he watched the preparations for a journey; yet should he proffer any suggestion about the horses or the manner of harnessing them, he dared to do so only with noticeable deference to the carter's own knowledge and ability, otherwise he would quickly have been told that "them as thinks they knows more about horses than I do, had better have as many years with 'em as I have and then p'raps they'd know a little".

An understanding ran between the carter and his horses which it was unwise to disturb. They had perfect confidence in him and he in them. They had never been removed from his influence; he had trained them, when they were wild colts, to work steadily, first in the plough team between older horses who were quite willing that they should exert their strengths to the full and, in consequence, do more than their share of the work; after that, in the cart and wagon, to custom them to the noise of the wheels and the feel of the shafts. They had surrendered their giant strengths to the carter's will; his intelligence was a solace to their temperaments; he was both guide and commander of their nervous doings.

He knew the years and times of their births; the sires and dams from whom their qualities had been inherited; he knew also their individual whims and dispositions and was always ready with the right word of encouragement and cheer. They shared a kind of language, a series of sounds peculiar to farm stable and plough land: *Heep! Heep! Haw! Gee! Woa! Comewit!* — perhaps the unchanged language of ancient horsemen, long since dead and forgotten. Each horse had its own name, to which it had also learned to respond; they were generally deep, full-sounding names. Should the plough team not be pulling in line, "Comewit, Smiler!" would bring Smiler back into the furrow, or "Gee, Dobbin!" would make old Dobbin ease to the right.

Only with horses was the carter happy, and he had inherited the love, for his father was a carter before him. As a boy he had listened to stories of his father's experiences, anecdotes of work on the land in which horse-management was always the real theme. To ride a horse then was his delight; and to sit on the wagon and hold the reins and the whip was his ambition. Growing up had only strengthened the bond; the horses that he had foaled, trained, and worked, formed the substance of his life-history.

That lifelong knowledge which it would have been an offence to question was his pride. It vibrated in his being as he sat on the front of the wagon, it travelled along the reins to the horses, who knew full well who was at the other end. The delicate check felt by their tender mouths, or the slight pull to right or left, accompanied by the familiar name and sound of command, inspired them with confidence. To them he was both commander and protector.

He had his beer allowance in his pocket and had already decided on the place where it would be spent. It was at crossroads, a house of call for many with a good "pull-up" space before it, and a long trough of water. Nose-bags were in the bed of the wagon, also cut chaff mixed with corn in a separate bag. For himself he had half of the top of a loaf and a wedge of boiled bacon. It was good to pull up there, to pass the strap of the nose-bag behind each horse's ears while the gratified mouths began to explore the contents. Good, too, to order the pint of mild, and above its foam to glance at their ripe forms, each horse happy with its feed. Not less was it his pleasant pride to note the admiring looks of others — neighbours of the countryside who chanced to be there — and to hear the brusque praise of his horses.

It was their day of show and his of joy, for only rarely did they leave the farm. With timid excitement they felt the hard road under their feet and heard the sounds of their own heavy hoofs pounding the flints. Each horse gave assurance to the other, and each shared the other's alarm. Nothing could quite uproot the wild instinct to flee from unusual sound or sight; their state hovered between their original wildness and their later training, and the carter's presence was the influence that constantly soothed and controlled them. Because they knew that he was there, the noise of the heavy wagon close behind them, the bump and grind of its heavy wheels over stones and ruts on the road, became as harmless as a lullaby.

Neither roads nor wagons were intended for hurrying journeys; only by railway could goods be moved quickly from place to place. It was boon enough to have a hard road to travel on, for only a few years had gone by since first they were lined with stones. It was not necessary now for the wheels to be nine inches thick, with separate rings of iron straikes nailed side by side on each — wheels that left behind a smooth pathway for foot passengers along the irregular surfaces of the lanes. Instead, wheels were now made only four inches wide, with a continuous iron tyre shrunken on. But there was still need now and then for brave pulls at the collar to drag the laden wagon over newly laid stretches of stones.

Such might have been the reflections in the carter's mind on the return journey to the farm. By the pitch of the horses' ears and the poise of their heads he knew that they were thinking again of their fellows at the farm. The empty wagon was as light as a toy to their combined strengths, their steps tended to increase in pace, it needed the check of the rein and his soothing command to prevent them from breaking into a run.

The milkers and those who tended the store cattle were of another and very different type. Their legs had not the four-square set of the carter's; the posture adopted when milking cows — an insecure squat on a three-legged stool, with a bucket pinched between the knees at the same time — left its effect in a widespread walk and slight curve of legs. They also inclined to a permanent stoop.

Their regard for the animals in their care was different from the carter's regard for his horses; because they were with them only during the times of milking and feeding, after which the cows were turned into the meadows to browse by themselves.

Indeed, to pass from the stable into the cowhouse was to enter another world altogether. Instead of the strong ammoniated smell of the stable, one became conscious of a pervading essence of meadows; the laxative quality of green grass in semi-fluid manure, and sweet-smelling milk. The breath of the cows was sweet with the grass they ate; the rhythmical getting of milk from the gently squeezed teats had its own series of musical notes; at first ringing on the bottom of the bucket; then changing to deeper and still deeper tones, and finally resolving into a luscious gurgle as the creamy volume deepened. The whole order of life there was measure and quietness. The walks of the cattle twice daily from pasture to cowhouse and back were slow and leisurely; and it was wise that the man in charge should dawdle, for each cow carried its heavy bag of milk, and to have hastened the pace would have reduced the flow. Their delicate udders were charged with the wealth of the valleys; it had been made through the long still hours of night, it was of the purity of the dew and the fragrance of the flowers.

The orderly ritual of milking was deeply expressive of man's union with nature through the beast, the process whereby the nutriment of the fields was made available to his need. It was a matter of give and take on both sides. Each cow knew that a feed of juicy pulped roots, mixed with chaff and meal, awaited her arrival at the cow-stall. It mattered little that for the time being her head was secured between two upright slats of wood, the enjoyment of food was a compensation that happened twice daily; all that was expected of her was a free yield of the milk that hung heavy and perhaps painfully in the bag. This, through the office of a good milker's hands, was a comfort to her, like the suck of the baby calf that had been taken away.

As with the horses, so with the cows, the farm and its fields was all their habitation, from which they had no need or desire to stray. They lived (and still continue to live) as kine have lived for centuries. No matter how much the methods of agriculture change for the quicker — and it is a policy of incessant speeding up — their ways and habits remain exactly the same.

The shepherd's duties took him from the farmstead to the fields far away, where his flocks of sheep were folded within hurdles on the fallow land. There, with his dog, he often worked for hours entirely alone. The solitude, and the responsibility and management of the flock, strongly developed his definite individuality. He lived and worked for his sheep, a supreme intelligence amid a crown of underlings whose lives and welfare were all subject to his control.

It was the farmer's duty to plan, and all the other labourers' duty to till the soil, to get the crops planted and grown, for the day when the shepherd would need them. He was the man who voiced the needs of a multitude of hungry mouths; his was the mind that looked ahead and forecast the demands that would have to be met. That responsibility made him a perpetual monitor of the farmer's life, a factor in the successful management of any farm.

So important were sheep to the welfare of the old English farm that the wise farmer gladly conceded the shepherd's imperative claims. It was not only value as mutton and wool that counted, but that systematic folding within hurdles had its direct result in good crops. Old labourers strongly favoured sheep farming, "It puts the crops straightway back into the land", they said, contrasting the system with the newfangled sending of produce away by rail, which they held to be folly. All agreed that the sheep should come first; which meant, as they understood, nothing less than that the shepherd had a right to his claims.

One such shepherd — old Jimmy — never hesitated to speak his mind to his master. Jimmy was a lifelong radical, and the farmer a lifelong conservative; yet, though wide apart even in politics, each held the other in high esteem.

The farmer proposed a change of food for the flock. "They be your sheep", Jimmy retorted, "an' you can do what you'd a-might with 'em, an' kill 'em all, for all I care; for that's what you be going to do, so I tell ye." And, of course, Jimmy was allowed to decide. It was out of the question to offend the old man.

Another time he arrived at the homestead in tears; the sheep were all ailing; he had tried everything, yet they still sickened, and he was at his wits' end. He was bidden not to take the trouble too much at heart, he had done his utmost, they said, and no man could do more.

One morning, in early June, I chanced to walk with him on his way to work. The sheep had all been shorn and were in a large fold on the rising ground in the distance. It was strangely cold for the time of year. Jimmy sighted the flock walking in a mass about the enclosure. "There they be", said he, "all frez-a-cold. They won't rest, nor *do* while this weather lasts."

The term "a-doing" was often on the lips of every Bucks labourer. They wanted their crops and animals to "do"; the endless trouble they took arose from this urgent desire of theirs; it could not have arisen from any mere consideration of the wage they received.

They understood the language of the animals on the farm and were able to recognize the cries of contentment or distress. The shepherd knew the cry of the lamb caught in a thicket and how it differed from the call for its mother. The stockmen who were in general charge of all the livestock knew at once the sounds denoting hunger or fright. To them the babel of the farmstead was a pleasing harmony or a call to action, and their movements were regulated accordingly.

CHAPTER
THREE

Work on the Land

Ploughing

The greater part of the soil was ploughed during the period between the end of harvest and March of the following year. Teams of horses, straining at the plough-chains and walking slowly to and fro across the bare fields, were the familiar sight of each winter, except when snow or severe frost held up all work.

As so much more of the land was then arable, it followed that far more men and horses were employed for the work — most of my school-fellows thought of the plough and general farm work as their careers in life. It is true that I have vivid remembrances of the heavy steam plough, with the giant engines, one on each side of the field, hauling the plough backwards and forwards between them by a strong wire-woven rope. But , apart from these — and they were not often seen — no other mechanical power was used for the cultivation of the soil.

A field was first evenly ploughed all over, after which cross ploughing — called *over-a-thurting* — often followed, severing the furrows and leaving the soil thoroughly exposed to the air. To plough a straight line crosswise over existing furrows demands, along with control of horses, a sense of direction so keen that at first thought it seems beyond explanation. It was done by keeping in sight some object on the far side towards which to steer. The straight furrow was the ploughman's pride, so was the straight line when seed corn was drilled. The horses themselves seemed to understand as much. The ploughman knew the dispositions of his horses and the extent to which he could rely on each of them. Their training was particularly noticeable at the end of a furrow, when a three-horse team was working. The leading horse (called the *for-ust*) by necessity would turn on reaching the hedge. Had they been acting on ordinary impulse, the other two horses would *at once* have followed the leader's example. But no! through their training each in turn kept straight on until precisely the same position was reached, then it turned. That was the only possible way to continue the furrow straight to the end.

The plough had its transforming effect on the landscape. Over large areas of pale stubble, rich bands of deep chocolate soil appeared, and slowly widened each day until the whole field was one uniform colour. It was good to view those large expanses of broken soil, and to know that by way of dew, sunshine, and showers the soil was being recharged with the powers of production.

How could man move amid that process, and have that vast operation taking place daily before his eyes, without having his whole life influenced by it? The farmer and his men understood that unison of the soil with the elements and recognized that they themselves were the agents through whom alone nature could fulfil that function. They knew that the horses and the plough, with their hands in control, were an essential part of an unchanging purpose that involved their thoughts and efforts. This understanding, which they expressed in their own way, was the source of the farmer's stable outlook on life, and of the labourers' patience and contentment.

Seed sowing

The bracing dry winds of March stirred up the activities of the district. Sometimes weather conditions in late February made work on the ploughed land even earlier. The soil became dry enough to be walked on and worked without kneading into a compound mass. It was found to be friable: the frosts of winter had broken it up; the hard clods of the preceding autumn were disintegrated, they crumbled before the scuffle and the harrows drawn over the surface by the horses.

The noise of the heavy horse-crush, the loud clang and clatter of its iron rings sounding on the hard road as it passed on the way to the fields, was a sign that spring, with seed sowing, was at hand. The sound always seemed to accord with the awakening of new life and activity that spread through the village. Every farm had its men and horses busy preparing and cleaning the soil; every cottage garden, or allotment, was being prepared for planting. The air of the lengthening evenings was charged with the smell of couch fires; they were dotted about over the far-spread fallows, each with a weak trail of smoke ascending into the crisp air.

When I was a boy, although the broadcasting of seed corn by hand had in general been superseded by the use of the horse-drawn drill, it still frequently happened that conditions favoured the ancient method. Furrows might lie in regular formation with the top soil dry, but too damp underneath to disturb. Over them the seed was cast and the whole surface harrowed to cover in the seed that had fallen into the deeps of the furrows.

Old men said that broadcasting was a better method: the seeds fell separately, they would say, and were all evenly distributed, whereas by the drill they were planted in rows, too close to each other. It was evident that no increase of crop was gained through its use.

The wheat had been sown during the late autumn of the preceding year — usually October. Over its fresh young growth, which spread away over large areas, men were busy plying the hoes. If the plant was weak, as sometimes happened with a rough winter, they plied the hoe to great advantage. Wheat has much recuperative power; it was good policy to tread on the emancipated growth and to cover it partially with soil, which caused it to tiller and expand over bare patches. When broadcasted by hand over neat furrows, the growth was in line almost as if planted by the drill; but on broken soil it was evenly distributed, and it seemed to me impossible that this all-over kind of crop could be hoed, yet old George — my instructor — declared that he had done so many times; that it was but a matter of working the hoe between the growths and treading and covering as the need was seen.

The men at hoeing worked amid advancing life, when every tree and bush was fringed with delicate colour, conscious that their work was done to encourage and nurture growth. George was sensitive to that, for he was wont to say — "I always think how beautiful the country is, when everything is coming into life again."

It relieved the farmer's mind to know that the corn crops were sown; his thoughts then turned to the preparation of the soil for the later sowing of seeds for the root crops.

Good crops of roots were essential to the well-being of the livestock. It was always a matter of planning provision for the winter that would follow, when many hungry mouths would have to be satisfied. Cultivation of roots meant much hard work, but no one seemed to grudge it. So soon as the tender young leaf was above soil, while it was still difficult to distinguish amid the weeds that had grown at the same time, the hoe began its work; first cleaning the spaces between the rows, and afterwards singling out the young plants. Repeated hoeings followed, which aerated the soil and stimulated the growth of the roots. It was commonly said that the crop could not be hoed too much, the work lasted through the summer, and provided a fall-back job when weather conditions were unsuitable for hay work.

The seed of the mangold-wurzel was the first to be sown. By comparison with swedes and turnips — which followed in succession — it was a modern crop to grow. George had a vivid remembrance of the first time that ever he saw the seed, when he and his fellow-workers had exclaimed at their odd shapes, so different from seeds of other roots. The milk-producing virtue of the wurzel soon made it popular, since when it has been regarded as the most important of root crops.

Haytime

On any well-regulated farm — and regularity is the outstanding characteristic of any well-managed farm — the approach of the longest day means that the crops of hay become the main consideration. The goodness of the grass, produced by growth, will by then be at its height; after the turn of days the crop will decline in quality.

The horse mower had appeared when I was a boy, but the scythe was still used for cutting many fields. To mow with a scythe meant harder labour than any man would willingly undertake to-day, yet the men of that time did not give them up without protest. They declared (and they were right) that cutting by scythe was cleaner, and that the after-growth was quicker; also, that where the crop lay almost flat the knives of the machine missed the lower halm, which remained uncut. On the other hand, it was evident that the machine left the crop more evenly and lightly spread over the field, whereas the scythe swept it into swathes which required shaking out afterwards. The horse mower has its own beauty of rhythm and grace of action, yet sentiment inclines to mowing by scythe as being more interesting and picturesque. Can any act of human labour excel the beauty of poise and sweep when a scythe is being swayed by a practised hand?

The men with scythes led the way in the old English hayfield. They worked in formation, one following the other, each cleaving a lane through the sea of waving grass and leaving it behind in a long billowy swathe. Their actions were precisely alike: an easy sweep from right to left, a graceful poise and movement of the whole body, the limbs in responsive unison of action. No doubt they had a pride of their skill, but it would have surprised them to be called perfect artists of their craft.

Those swathes were taken in hand by women wearing granny bonnets tied under the chin, who followed with forks and tossed the new-mown grass in the air, making it separate in the air and fall lightly, well distributed over the ground. Their aim was to bring it all into contact with the sun and air and to leave no space of ground un-covered. This was called *tedding*.

That light carpet of mown grass was then allowed to lie in the sun until the top layer had dried, when over the field stole a subtle fragrance denoting that it was changing to hay. Only by the sun's warm rays could its perfection of sweetness be attained. This the workers always acknowledged: "Do what we will", said they, "the sun is the true haymaker."

The women's work was not only to turn the hay so that the sun might dry it thoroughly, but also by degrees to draw it together into rows for the convenience of carrying. After the new-mown grass had all been tedded, they changed their forks for wooden rakes and so walked together in formation round and round the field, drawing the partially dried grass into small rows, called *leeks* or *windrows*. These they turned and re-turned, as the need was seen, sometimes at the same time drawing two rows into one. The raking always brought the undried grass lying at the underside of the rows into exposure; at the same time it took account of the final need, gradually bringing all the hay up into large rows at convenient distances apart for the hay carts.

If it was held to be unsafe to risk the shower that might fall in the night, the half-made hay, lying in large rows, was often made into cocks. In them it was fairly safe, even if the weather changed for the worse. The well-built cock was like a thatched cube of hay, the top layers discharging the rain to the outside; and little water fell on the area of a cock by comparison with the amount that would have fallen on the same quantity of hay in a row. It was wisest to make these cocks while the hay was warm with the sun. The hay kept warm throughout the night, and the heat developed a kind of humidity that quickly disappeared when, the following morning, the cock was turned and shaken up. After evaporation the hay so treated was often found in condition to be carried.

The heavier work of the hayfield was done by the men, who loaded the carts and wagons in the field and unloaded them and built the ricks either in a corner of the field or at the farmyard. Sometimes the women followed close behind the pitchers, cleaning up the leavings with hand-draft rakes; this prevented overdrying of the hay, as happens when the whole field is left to be raked after carrying is done. But as often as not they were in the next field, tedding the mown grass behind the mowers again.

To ride on a load of hay from the field to the farm was then a proper theme for verse and song. It is doubtful if the luxury can be equalled; that laying oneself flat on its warm responsive bed to breathe its sweetness in, to rest the body tired with toil. The consciousness was of being borne altogether above matters of earth; neither horse nor wagon could be seen; they were below, hidden by the flat bulk of hay. Only the rhythmical thud of the horse's feet came up, or the carter's full-throated command and the "clap, clap" of the ponderous wooden wheel stocks as they turned on their axles. The jolt when the springless wheels passed over uneven ground was made pleasant by the soft bed on which one lay. It was a short surrender to perfect ease, a glad yielding to a swaying movement, with only the blue sky and white fleecy clouds above to watch one's well-deserved spell of laziness. The passing from the field to the lane was known by the turn and movements peculiar to the gateway; the lane itself was an experience of alternating sun and shade, and a trail of leaves from overhanging branches that lightly brushed the load as it passed.

Haytime was the first ingathering, and was made much of in the sentiment of old country life. Much less land was then grass-grown, and the hay crop was cherished and tended, therefore, to a degree that has not been usual since. It was wanted almost wholly for feeding the livestock through the coming winter, and no time or attention was ever grudged to get it in in good condition.

I heard the tales that old men told of pre-enclosure days, when only the long meads that skirted the streams were allowed to remain under grass. On these meads the common holders of arable strips had rights of mowing, and when the crop was ripe for cutting they would assemble to cast lots for the portion that each should have. One in whose integrity they all had confidence was chosen to act as master of ceremonies. He first of all gathered dock leaves, which he cut into known shapes — *hog*, *trough*, *crowsfoot* and other now-forgotten forms — each to stand for a part of the meads known by that name. The leaf fragments, cut to numbers and shapes, were shaken all together in a hat, and a boy was appointed to draw them singly and to hand them in order to the holders of mowing rights. But before the drawing was done, the head-man always shouted "Hark-ho" three times in succession, and recited a rigmarole — now forgotten — which called all present to witness that the lots were drawn without fear or favour.

The ceremony, they said, never varied. Each holder, when by his shapen dock leaf he knew the lot of grass it was his fortune to have, was obliged to be content, whether the tract was good or bad. The lot holders called for the services of boys, who always attended. These boys, they said, would be taken to one side of the broad stretch of mead, stationed at the dividing points, and told to look beyond to the other side, each to some special tree or other recognized distinguishing mark. To this they were to run through the long grass — three boys, one behind the other; strict command was given to the leader to keep his eyes on the mark to which he was running, so that the track of trodden grass should be as straight as he could make it. Those were the boundaries to which the mowers mowed.

The order of this ceremony continued unchanged until the enclosure of 1830. It is not difficult to guess at the picturesque assembly of yeomen in the early hours of a day of late June. They all carried their scythes, with drink and provender for the day; and after lots had been drawn, each started to mow the part of the mead that had fallen to him; the day having been put off until, by country weather-wisdom, a spell of good weather had been forecast, because apart from the little they could cut from the baulks, paths and lanes that abutted their arable strip, they depended entirely on these meads for their year's supply of hay.

A century of years of change separates us from that scene, with its music of many steel blades being sharpened. It all belongs to a vanished past, to a set of simple and sturdy men, all gone now, yet to whom we still owe our best ideals and aspirations. To run a track, straight and true, was the ambition of those boys; and it somehow helps me to know that the son of the last boy to run a track for the village still lives as I write.

Corn harvest

When the exhilaration of June had passed and the brilliance of July was merging into the sultry heat of August, then all the attention of the village turned to the harvest. Great fields of corn spread away on every hand; its ripening was made manifest by the wide change-over from green to bronze and gold, and the air itself was charged with a subtle change — the smell of dying herbage.

The harvest was the goal to which the main efforts of the past year had been directed; its ingathering was all-important to the village. The laying down of arable land to grass began when I was a boy; yet corn was still so widely grown that at harvest it was impossible to escape the harvest redolence that pervaded all the district. The horse-drawn reaping machine had appeared, with its four spreading sails that dropped obliquely in succession to sweep a sheaf of cut corn aside. Its use had eased the growing problem of hand labour, which, before I was born, had become so pressing that the carpenters and wheelwrights left their benches, the masoners laid down their trowels, and all others left their crafts to help to get the precious corn in. If they had not gone (so it was said) the farmers would have withheld their patronage during the ensuing winter. The enclosure had brought a much larger area of land into cultivation each year, and never before had the need of help been so great.

Farming methods did not change so quickly then, and as long as labour was available at an economic price, the farmers did not favour machines. Cutting by hand was clean and effective, whether the crop was standing or partially laid by gales, and the hand-cut-and-bound sheaf fitted its neighbour in the shock in a way to keep the rain out. Sentiment was strong, too: the cottagers regarded the work as their right; cutting the corn was the big event of their year, a task anticipated and arranged for. It was their opportunity of earning a few extra pounds; and not

41

to have this extra money would have meant something like chaos to their carefully planned lives.

Whole families planned for work in the harvest field: the father with the eldest children, to go daily in advance; the mother, with those younger, to follow later, with provender for the day. The work was done by the piece; it was a matter of slaving from morn to late evening, an incessant "slash, slash", with the gleaming fagging hook at the ripe corn; and then the gathering of the severed halm together and the binding of it with a straw band laid ready on the ground by one of the children. The work was called "fagging", a truly descriptive title, in contrast to the earlier method of cutting with a sickle, which was called "reaping".

The fagging hook differed from the sickle. It was of heavier make, for it had to sever the halm close to the ground, with a strong swinging slash: whereas the lighter sickle severed the straws about half-way up. The reaper with a sickle passed the curved blade round a portion of standing corn and drew it towards himself; the pull made the ears cluster in a bunch, which he gripped, and severed the straws immediately afterwards. Tucking the cut corn under his left arm, he repeated the action until he had enough to make a sheaf. Reaping by sickle had served the needs when storage in barns and threshing by flails was general. It was an advantage that the sheaves were small, because more could then be stored inside. But when straw was wanted for thatching, it was cut close to the ground.

Throughout harvest time, an unusual quietness, a sense of desertion, reigned in the village, broken only by the occasional passing of a wagon laden with corn from the fields. Old men, too old for harvest work, stood at their cottage gates to see them go past; the healthy and strong were away in far fields, and did not come back to the village until evenfall. Then, in the long twilight that brought down the still autumn nights, the village awakened to activity; then, straggling families, dead tired, wended their ways to their cottage homes, to supper and to sleep. Sticks gathered for firing lay alongside the baby asleep in the pram; a glow appeared in the small lattice windows, and the smell of fry penetrated the evening air.

On Saturdays they ceased work earlier; Saturday was the day for a *sub* on the work done. Then each public house was a babel of voices within, with a song at times. Each little village shop was busy; the butcher's cleaver sounded on the block as he chopped the joints of "fresh meat" — as they called it, in contrast to the usual salt bacon — for the Sunday dinner.

On Monday, if it was fine, they were back at their tasks in their allocated portions of the field, called *drifts*. Some faggers had forged ahead of others; and a half-cut crop then had a zigzag look, very different from the half-cut crop of to-day. The *drift* of the expert cutter was often a wide alley cut through the middle of the expanse; and looking across, only the heads and shoulders of the workers could be seen, rising and falling as they cut and bound the sheaves, like bathers in a golden sea.

What bath there was, however, was of sweat from the worker's body; a continuous, healthy moisture that dried all day in the heat. Sweat and sun together hardened the skin, which became deeply tanned where it was uncovered, and graduated to a lighter colour where it was protected by the loosely worn shirt. The muscles of the arms were as knotted ropes, their skins hardened through contact with hard, ripe straws. The worker felt himself impervious, sinewy and alert; one who, in spite of the heavy toil and the little pay, rejoiced in the excellent doing of it.

No wonder the noonday rest came to them like nature's own blessing, which made a feast indeed of the simple fare. The crust of home-baked bread crackled in the grip of strong teeth; the clinging fat of the home-fed bacon stuck to the knife; but in the mouth together they formed a masticated compound that pleased the palate and satisfied hunger.

Then followed the greatest blessing of all. Under a shady tree the stubble became an easy bed and the cut sheaf of corn a kind pillow. Sleep now; surrender to the claims of a tired body; forget all the matters of the moment; yield to an influence like good motherhood that enfolds the whole being in one embrace! This was Nature's answer to the needs of these children of hers, whose lives had never been separated from the soil. The overhanging leaves screened the heat of the high sun; a light breeze fanned the bronzed cheeks as thus they slept.

The drifts cut by the faggers varied in size; if they were to be properly measured definite marks were needed on the stubble after the crop had been carried. These marks were made simply by tying half a dozen straws of rooted corn together in a knot, and cutting off the ears. Knotted bunches like this were seen dotted all over the stubble after the corn had been carted. They were there, as everyone knew, to guide the land-measurer when he should come to measure the work done by each fagger.

The measurer was usually a man of the village; one who had learned to read and write and to cast up figures. He was a go-between, and employer and worker each had confidence in him. He measured up the areas (often irregular in shape) cut by each worker, rendered a return to the farmer, and on the basis of this measurement payment was made. The farmers paid over his fees to him, but deducted half of the amount from the workers' earnings.

The land-measurer's task involved much walking to and from distant farms, also over the fields when he got there. As soon as he arrived a man was told off to go with him, to draw the long chain with which the drifts were measured and to give the names of the workers who had cut them. They had already drawn subs on the work done, and awaited his statement of what was still due to them. With harvest money the thrifty labourer's wife made many payments and purchases; especially boots for the husband and children against the coming winter.

A word must be said of the gleaners. They assembled at the gateway of the first field of wheat to be carried and went in as the last load left the field.

Mothers with children and pram were there, and widows and spinsters, all prepared to spend long hours walking and re-walking the sunburned stubble, picking up the corn singly as it was found. Those single ears they arranged into a bunch held by the left hand; when the bunch was too large to hold, it was tied with a straw and placed aside until evening, or until the field had been scoured. Those neat bunches were eventually made up into one large sheaf, beautifully shaped as a large rosette of ripe ears of wheat, and proudly carried home to the cottage.

It is impossible to over-estimate the value of that gleaned corn to the very poor. Gleaning, too, afforded at least one example of communal spirit surviving the enclosure; it was acknowledged as a customary right, though it had no legal basis. Farmers were not blind to the value of the waste corn as food for the herd of young pigs, or flock of poultry, which have taken the place of gleaning in later years. No one, at the time I write of, denied the privilege or would have risked the opposition of public opinion if it had been withheld.

At the time of my youth it was usual for the wheat stubble only to be gleaned; the farmers turned young pigs on to that of barley and beans. But the record of one man — told to me — suggests that formerly they also were gleaned. He said that he and his mother and two other children gleaned during one harvest a total of twelve bushels of wheat, five of barley, and two of beans; he said that she would rise at four in the morning and return at seven with her first large bundle of corn; then, after breakfast, accompanied by her children, they would all glean until late evening — sixteen hours for her of back-aching toil.

Corn so gained was hardly earned; but those who gleaned it knew that they had secured what would stand them in good stead against the privations of the coming winter. Those cottagers knew all that is to be known about thrift; they spent long hours in the evenings or on wet days rubbing out the corn from the ears by hand, or thrashing them on the cottage floor with a stick. They carried the mingled corn and husk to a windy place where, tossed in the air, the chaff was carried away; or, at times, it was cleaned of chaff by the bellows from the fire. The cleaned corn was taken to the mill to be ground; and the miller generally arranged a special grinding for gleaner's corn, a few days before the village feast.

The pulling of bean stubble for the fire had almost ceased when I was a boy. Once only my brother and I helped a widow pulling it in the field. She gave us a few coppers for our trouble and my mother scolded us for accepting them.

Harvest over, the village settled down again to normal life. The hum of the threshing machine sounded, first at one farm, then at others. But not many years before it had been a matter of flails sounding from every barn, of which there were scores then that no longer exist. My father said that when walking the mile which is the length of the village, you could not get away from the sound; as the "thump! thump!" was lost from one barn, it was heard from the next in succession, and so on from end to end of the village.

In those days, when corn was cut by the sickle, much halm or straw was left on the fields. Should the weather continue fine after harvest, men were sent to mow it with the scythe. They did not give the long sweep from right to left as when mowing grass; but stopped the cut in front of the left foot, with which they pushed the cut halm along until enough had accumulated to make what they called a "wad" — that is, as much as could conveniently be picked up with a fork. This second cutting they called "bagging the halm". It was carted to the farms and used for litter for the livestock; or it served for packing up the roof on the horizontal timbers when making an over-layer hovel. This old type of farm shed is still sometimes called "the halm hovel", and when one happens to be pulled down to-day the short lengths of straw, cut in the days of the sickle and the ancient systems of husbandry, may still be found within its roof.

CHAPTER
FOUR

The Village Crafts

The native crafts of a village are a profitable study; for they reveal how happily man has adopted, in his efforts to obtain a livelihood, some service to his fellows. They reveal his creative instinct, and often, still further, that urge of his to make the creation of his hands not only useful but also beautiful. Often, too, studied in their place, the local crafts reveal how man has adopted some special provision natural to the locality — the clay, the stones, the subsoil, or the growths that most abound — to serve his needs. This local use of nature's provisions has given to many villages a definite character that may still be recognized.

Although agriculture, in my own village, was the basis of its prosperity, almost all the other crafts essential to rural life were carried on within its bounds. Some built the houses and kept them in repair, and others made the clothes and boots that the people wore. There were blacksmiths and saddlers and hurdle-makers and plough-makers and wheelwrights and thatchers.

We may believe that each craft was almost as old as the village, and that each had developed at the same pace. That each came into being in response to a need; in fact, that when the early settlers found it necessary to have a shelter from the rain and cold, some of them were more able in making such things and by ability became the acknowledged builders to the community. So, we may suppose, had the tailor, the bootmaker, and the rest of the craftsmen become established. Certainly each had developed special abilities that had been handed down from fathers to sons over the years and each had given the workers separate personalities, so that, even in my time, when a man was mentioned, we always saw him in association with his particular craft, and respected him according to his thoroughness in it.

Through their knowledge and abilities made the craftsmen independent of work on the land for a livelihood, yet the soil was, indirectly, the source of their income too. The needs of the farms brought them the largest part of their business, and so the greater part of what they earned passed through the farmers' hands before it reached their pockets. This left the farmers in authority: theirs was finally the rule to which all the villagers conformed.

Work at a craft was deemed to be superior to working on the soil, an idea that had little or no justification, except that the earnings were slightly better and that uniqueness of ability gave a kind of preserve to the possessors. Everybody seemed to know something of the ins and outs of agriculture, whereas the craftsman, by comparison, was ensconced in a private knowledge of his craft. In that respect he certainly had something that the others had not, and he gained respect thereby.

To the genuine agriculturists, all the village craft workers, one might say, were as cousins once removed.

Before the enclosure, their forefathers had all held plots, and had cultivated them along with their crafts; and the love of the land thus formed had by no means died. They might be proud of what they knew of their crafts, but the ambition of many of them was to get back to the soil, and to farm on their own. Some compromised, cultivating a rod or two of land and breeding a few head of livestock, alongside of the business of their crafts.

Building

The early builders wisely and necessarily looked to the neighbourhood for their building materials. They felled the oak saplings and cleft their trunks. With the quarters so obtained, they built their houses, the walls framed in panels, and each opening filled with wattled sticks and daubed with mortar. Their roofs they covered with straw from the land, in plenteous layers, thick and impervious to either heat or cold. They built to their own need and liking, unvexed by any authority other than the manorial rule under which the sites were granted, the concern of which was limited to the fulfilment of services and dues relevant to the grants.

It was discovered that nature had made generous provision for the village: just under the soil a deep layer of a chalk-like mixture was to be found in plenty with which good sound walls could easily be built. Although the earliest homes were built of timber and wattle and daub, it is evident that that method was discarded when this discovery was made.

The manner of using it was simple, and came naturally to habitual users of forks and spades. It needed treatment similar to that for soil: being excavated early in winter, so that the frosts should break it down, and it was then ready to be used for building when the birds began to build their nests. To prepare it for use it was soaked with water, then turned and trodden until it reached the consistency of dough, after which, with a little straw mixed in to hold it together till dry, it was ready to erect.

The method of building was equally simple. The only tool used was a short, flat-pronged fork. With this, the builder stood in position on the stone-built foundation. From a heap of the prepared "clay" that lay alongside the foundation, his mate dug a forkful and deposited it on the fork of the builder, held ready before him. The builder immediately turned it over and patted it into position. They repeated this until a "berry", that is, a layer some eighteen inches high by sixteen inches thick, was formed the length of the foundation. The builder stepped backwards as the berry advanced: its sides were left uneven at first; it was left like this a few days to dry out a little, and was then chopped straight and smooth with the spade.

The villager made good use of this handy material: for years they built with little else, not only houses to live in, but also stables and sheds for their horses and cattle. When Nonconformity appeared, two meeting-places were also built in the same way. The supply was inexhaustible, and all to be had for the digging; and so having built their houses and outhouses, they turned to the boundaries of their properties and enclosed them in high walls of the same stuff, covering them with neat roofs of thatch to keep out the weather. No town-planning scheme hampered their efforts; each man built to his own sweet will until at last the village became a curious maze of walls and narrow ways where often the stranger walks in perplexity even yet.

Nowhere else in England, they say, can so many miles of walls be found. A more primitive method of building can hardly be imagined — and the bricklayer from other parts is plainly mystified by it — yet many walls erected centuries ago may be seen as substantial to-day as when first built; some have their sides plastered or covered with rough cast; and a few reveal Elizabethan decoration.

The material is peculiar to the district, and is known by its local name *wichert* or *wichut*. The walls afford an example of an ancient use of local material holding its own until quite recent times.

The village workmen, because they built with stones and wichert far more often than with bricks, were known as *masoners*. Masoners were homely folk, content with long hours and small wages, but a class slightly above the farm labourers because of their independence. Like the farm hands they wore corduroy trousers, though not so invariably tied under the knees. We — the carpenters — walked long distances with them, to and from the work on hand. Their clothes smelt of lime, whereas ours were said to smell of wood, though we were not conscious of it. They never blacked their boots, which in parts were light grey through contact with wichert and lime, and in more prominent places, especially the toes, rubbed to the inner brown of the leather. They carried their trowels, their pitchen and stone hammers, their fibre brush and pair of lines, together with their beavor and dinner fare, also drink, all in a flag-woven basket slung over the shoulder by a leathern strap, and counter-balanced by the plumb-rule at the other end. These walks were often in the gloaming, before or after daylight, and at times in darkness so deep that when the way lay over pathless fields, the remembered form of a dark elm alone served for direction. To emerge from those dark fields on to the well-trodden ways of our own village was a relief to me like a traveller's return to civilization.

Those masoners well understood the lore of their own craft. They knew the subsoils (of clay) that needed wide foundations, and those on which they could build with greater confidence. They knew the separate qualities of the bricks and limes that were burnt at the kilns near at hand. For mortar they used the scrapings from the flint roads and the trimming of the verges, called "sidings". During winter the roads were scraped and their verges cut; the material so obtained was placed in heaps on the grass borders and sold by the mile by the local authority. Its quality varied according to the amount of soil that had been taken on to the roads by the wheels of farm carts coming off the fields. This was known and noted and allowed for by the masoners when they made their purchases.

Their work was of rural excellence, strong and unpretentious; it included not only wichert, but bricks and mortar and all that was akin to these. They laid pitched stone paths along many of the zigzag ways of the village. Folk then, of course, wore thick, hobnailed boots, and did not mind the projecting stones that have worried the corns of later generations. Masoners were also prepared to sink a well, blasting out the thick beds of rock that lay under the strata of wichert and lining it with a circular *steening* of stones laid without mortar; or to build a bridge over a stream. They had their own elementary systems of drainage (this was before the day of the glazed socket-pipe) and knew how to contrive what they called "stink-traps", brick chambers with a slate edgewise at the centre, the object of which was to keep the gas from the cesspool from returning along the drain (the method of conducting it to the air above by vent pipes had not then been thought of). The channels they formed with half-round, butt-jointed pipes, which were laid, one below, and one on top, to complete the cylinder, a system that allowed the top half to be lifted for cleansing purposes. A long drain, to carry water only, might sometimes be made with flat stones pitched together at top. This was called a *shock drain*.

The carpenter's business was quite separate from the masoner's, and so, also, were the painter's and the decorator's, though all three crafts often worked together on a job that needed them all. The combination of all building crafts into one concern was being adopted in the towns nearby, but had not reached the villages. I had relatives in each of the three crafts, and they therefore undertook work as a family concern, but each was responsible for a separate department. It seems to me that the separateness gave greater dignity to each craft. There was the master masoner, the master carpenter, and the master painter, who also did plumbing and glazing. They sometimes grumbled at one another's management, if it did not happen to fit in with their own; but on the whole the system answered — time was not quite the tyrant then that it is now.

The Carpenters

The master carpenter attended sales of timber to buy in oak, elm, and firs. These were sawn at his own pit, and the planks from them were stacked until dry enough for use. It was necessary to look well ahead and maintain a stock: large butts had to lie one year before sawing; and planks and boards had to season one year for each inch of their thickness. This storage of butts and planks in the carpenter's yard gave the business a look of stability that is much rarer to-day.

The sawyers' work at the pit went on the whole year round. They were a separate class of woodworkers, and knew the special needs of both carpenters and wheel-wrights; how to cut wide boards for coffins; and narrow feather-edged, for the walls of farm buildings; they knew the proper dimensions of gate posts and all the varied sizes for the separate parts of field gates. All this, together with quite other sizes of planks and boards, which the wheelwright wanted. Their service was indispensable to old English woodwork. When it was common it was taken for granted; yet, to-day, because it is a thing of the past, it seems imbued with rich value.

The sawyers worked amid a litter of chips, a redolent carpet of sawdust under their feet. It was a process centuries old, and it seemed destined to go on for all time. The sharpening of the saw had its own musical rhythm, and so had its up and down swing at the pit. The sawyers were rugged men of great masculine strength; their action at work — the high fling of the bared arms that grasped the handles of the gleaming saw, and their swift descent — was a dramatic symbol of Man's mastery over the material things of nature, his ability to convert its provisions to his own use.

The workshop doors opened straight on to the timber yard. Through them the seasoned timbers were carried, to re-emerge as parts and finished articles — doors and windows for houses, gates for the fields, cow-cribs for the stockyards, and long wooden troughs for the sheepfolds. The shop was a palace of craft in which rough wood was shaped, fitted, and tamed, to serve the needs of man and beast. It was a building of antiquity, dim-lit, and dedicated to that special purpose. Its music was the sound of tools and the voices of men working well together: its whole air was charged with the smell of wood.

It was, so to speak, the temple of carpentry; and seven years of apprenticeship was not thought too long to study and learn its secrets. The double ambition of every apprentice was to possess a complete set of tools and to excel in the craft. They saw in an article of beauty the reflection of its maker's character; its excellence and his were one.

Painters

The painters were the aristocrats of the crafts; their work was lighter, and they wore cloth trousers. It was they who put the final appearance to the carpenters' work, and to the walls and ceilings that the masoners had plastered. The dust and dirt created by carpenters or masoners was abomination to the painters who, when they arrived on the job, wanted everyone else to clear off and leave them to themselves.

They formerly prepared their own paints by rubbing down dry powder colours in oil on a flat stone: they also made their own varnish from gums which they dissolved in turpentine. The ability to make paint or varnish of tone and texture that would withstand extremes of temperature and weather was the basis of each man's reputation as a craftsman. He was often the reputed owner of secret recipes for wood stains and distemper washes, and he was careful to keep such a reputation.

The painters also did all the plumbing and glazing. Before I knew them, but not long before, they had actually cast their own sheet lead for gutters, valleys, and angles of roofs; as well as the lead pumps that were superseding the more ancient pumps of wood. They still cast and milled the lead for lattice windows. Even after it could be purchased ready-made, the best of them continued to use their own; for the delicate strips were easily damaged in transit, and this damage made the window-making more difficult. To possess a diamond gave them mastery in the art of cutting glass. Wisely, they refused to lend it, because a glazier's diamond in some mysterious way accommodates itself to a particular user, and having been used by a borrower, takes a long time to resume a correct action for its owner.

The Wheelwrights

Though the wheelwrights were separate from the carpenters, much of their work was common to both crafts. They, also, bought timber in advance; they, also, sawed it at the pit and seasoned it for several years before use; many of their tools were the same and were used after the same manner. But the work had peculiarities, and their methods differed, for the reason that little or no carpenters' work would be asked to withstand the strains to which the wheels and bodies of carts and wagons were subjected. The wood used by wheelwrights had to be stronger — tough and flexible. English ash has these qualities; and this was the timber mainly used by wheelwrights. The carpenter rarely had ash in his workshop at all. The cart or wagon was built to be a compact body, a unity of parts rigidly framed together, so that, even when heavily loaded, it would withstand the shocks and jolts of uneven roads. Each separate piece was made to size and shape, precisely according to the strain to which it would be subjected. Each part was also shaped to curves convenient and pleasing; the shafts to fit comfortably to the shape of the horse, and the body to suit the work and purpose for which it was made.

From start to finish the construction of the old English cart or wagon must have demanded an alert mind, a trained eye, and mature judgement. Years of experience and tradition were the wheelwrights' teachers; yet the need for thoroughness of execution and quality of materials was constant and demanded from each craftsman, however long in experience, the same watchful care. The wheelwright was indeed an artist, whose soul was in his handiwork and whose pride of life was vested in the soundness and beauty of the things he made.

Each wheel he made, for example, was nothing less than a unity, of stock, spokes, and felloes of wood, seasoned to the last degree of perfection, rigidly framed together, and bound firm at last with a strong iron tyre. Each wheel had to be built to turn easily without wobble, and to stand incessant jolts and strains. Only perfection of workmanship made this possible; from start to finish nothing might be scamped, each joint must fit exactly, the parts being finally driven together by a heavy sledge wielded by strong arms.

Those wheels were built for the roads and changed with them. My father told me of the days before roads were all lined with stones, when — so he said — the heavy wagon had wheel-rims so wide that the tracks they left behind formed convenient footpaths. Such wide heavy wheels must have involved an even higher degree of skill in their making; so that, even in the days of my youth, the wheelwrights' was a declining art.

A friendly rivalry existed between the wheelwrights and the carpenters, which found its expression sometimes in harmless banter. They thought their craft superior and said so. Our retort was simply "paint and putty". Someone told me that a poor wheel wright might make a good carpenter, but that it needed an exceptionally good carpenter to make a poor wheelwright.

The Hurdle-makers

The craft of the hurdle-makers had an interest of its own. They worked with primitive tools — the axe, saw, drawing-knife, and shell-bit, and they had one special tool, used by no other woodworkers, with which they removed the centre of the mortices. This was called "the hurdle-maker's tool".

The hurdles in our neighbourhood were made of the branches of the willows that bordered the streams, an adaptation of local material for local need. The willows were lopped during winter, the larger branches were split down the middle, and sheep hurdles were made of the separated halves. The tool used for splitting was called a "frammer"; it was knocked in with a lump of wood, and the cleft was continued straight down the middle by levering the handle of the frammer.

All the methods of the hurdle-makers were rudimentary, yet very quick and effective. They did not wait to season the wood but used it in its sappy condition, chopping the cleft poles with the axe and shaping them with the drawing-knife. Their methods seemed to be survivals of ancient carpentry, before planes and other improved tools were made. The tenons were chopped and fashioned in the same manner to a slight taper, so that they would tighten when driven into the mortice, where they were held in position by nails.

The convenient size and design of the hurdle was decided long ago, and there has been no deviation since. They are still made the same to-day; they serve a definite purpose, and no improvement is possible. In that respect they are one feature of old English life still with us unchanged, although, since the folding of sheep on fallows is now more rare, their use is consequently much less than formerly.

Plough-makers

Plough-making of wood was formerly a craft separate to itself; its ancient recognition is suggested by a wooden plough carved on the bench end of our village church. But the last plough-maker of our village, Benjamin Montague, died at the time of my boyhood. Ploughs made by him had the reputation of being well made and easy to use; and auctioneers would quote his name to inspire biddings when a plough of his happened to be in their sale. The furrow cleanly turned and straight was the ploughman's pride; no ploughman hesitated to express his dislike of an awkward plough when it was his fate to have to handle one. Nor was the maker too far away to hear of the remarks; the men who made them were near at hand; their reputation rose or fell accordingly.

One has only to think of the intense strain to which a plough was necessarily subjected — two or three strong horses, using all their strength to draw it forward through stiff soil — to know the need of good construction. Nor was it only a matter of sturdiness; a good plough must be designed and formed to turn the soil evenly. The secret was largely in the shaping of the broad board and in the general arrangement of the handles so as to give the ploughman full power of control.

The broad board was sawn out from a lump of wood; and I well remember a master wheelwright saying that "few men knew how to do it". Those that knew owed the knowledge partly to long experience, and perhaps also partly to inheritance.

When I was young the making of wooden ploughs was already a declining art. Ploughs of iron were taking their place; yet until quite recently a few farmers have preferred them for use on water-logged soils.

Blacksmiths

No village would be complete without its blacksmith's shop. Ours had several. The smiths' main job was the shoeing of horses for the farms and the village, but they undertook anything in iron work.

Their workshops had a character and glamour that belonged to no other craft: a dim-lit smoky atmosphere, enlivened by the ruddy fire and hot glowing iron. From within a dusky recess, the large bellows emitted its deep breath as the handle was moved up and down, meantime a curious chuckle of valves sounded, in reality its action of taking breath, though it seemed to be the bellows' acknowledgement of its own part in the work that was going forward. A cowhorn was fixed on the end of the handle; its curve was comfortable to the blacksmith's hand; it remained clean where everything else was grimy.

The smith had his own peculiar way of working that bellows: a persuasive pressure downwards, regulated to give the strength of blast that the fire exactly needed.

The smith knew what was wanted because he was a smith; his thought pierced the molten deeps of the fire and knew the transformation that was taking place there; he judged the heat required for mere shaping, or for the more subtle process of welding or joining two pieces of iron together, and knew the precise moment when it must be withdrawn from the fire and held on the anvil, ready for the blows of his hammer.

Every morning soon after six the sound began — the music that, floating over intervening fields, at times roused us from slumber. "Bong-ha! Bong-ha! Bong-ha! Bong-ha! Bong! Bong! Bong!" We knew that they were shaping iron shoes in readiness for the horses that would soon arrive; that the smith with his hammer, and a strong youth wielding a sledge, stood, one each side of the anvil, beating a hot bar of iron into shape. The youth already had muscles on his arms that we envied; he was proud of his strength and the skill that he was attaining. It appealed to our sense of manhood that he was not afraid to lift the heavy feet of those horses and to pare their hoofs, also that he was able to swing that heavy sledge with such ease and precision of strike.

All the village seemed to need the service of the blacksmiths. They repaired the implements of the farms; they made hoes for the labourers; at hay and harvest time men went to them for new scythes and fagging hooks; or to have their old ones ground to the new edge on the grindstone. At those special times the smith's shop was a place of meeting, where one could learn how work was going in distant parts of the large parish. The grindstone was hardly dry all day and the smith was always ready to adjust the hang of a scythe, or to make a fagging hook fast again in its wooden handle.

He also shaped the rings and inserted them in the noses of the cottagers' pigs, to prevent them routing up the floors of the sties. The wives carried their leaky kettles, pots, and pans to his shop for repair; and as children we went to him for rolling hoops, which he made of half-inch rolled bar and sold at the modest price of fourpence.

He also made the curious three-pronged forks, with flat tines, with which the masoners built the wichert walls of the village. They were a local necessity, and could not be bought at any ironmonger's shop. Few days passed at my father's carpentry shop without some need of blacksmith's work — hinges with side wings attached, for field gates and large barn doors, called hooks and thimbles; catches, keepers, hasps and staples, and many other odd items of ironwork. As a boy it was often my job to run those errands of necessity, and I loved to wait and watch the roaring fire and the smith's methods of work. Yet the iron which they handled so freely, and shaped so easily to size or curve, afterwards seemed harsh and cold to my hands. It had not the responsive feel to which I was already accustomed with the handling of wood.

Bootmakers

The boot and shoe makers were a busy folk, for the "ready-made" had not appeared for sale in the village and almost all the village boots were made to order and to measure. My father told me that before I was born there was a time when cobblers' work made employment for forty men and youths. Very likely they served other smaller places round the village; probably, too, they made the long leathern gaiters worn by thatchers, hedgers, and carters.

Many, however, made only heavy boots for work on the land; boots of bark-tanned leather, of ponderous size, the soles hand-stitched and studded with rows on rows of large hobnails. The lace-holes had no brass eyelets and the tongues were stitched to the uppers, which gained them the title and reputation of "water-tights". These workshops smelt of cobblers' wax and leather, to which my nose, accustomed to the smell of wood, was sensitive.

Each worker seemed ensconced in the dignity of his own craft ability, to which I, a mere onlooker, felt an outsider. It was with admiration that I watched the deft cutting out of uppers and sole pieces on the soft cutting-board of poplar, and the subsequent stitching on of the soles; the exact piercing with the curved shining awl, its passage made easier by a preceding dip into the greasepot; the two waxed threads passed in opposite ways through the hole and vigorously pulled tight to right and left. Each stitch audibly announced its reliable grip in response to that powerful pull, and remained embedded comfortably in the light tanned leather, one of a curved serrated row, with glutinous brown top, in shape and placing exactly like the others.

Each farm labourer had his favourite maker, one who had made his boots for him before — good boots that had withstood the tests of wet and snow, and had been renewed more than once by heeling and soling. To be "dry-a-foot" was a wise maxim of theirs, and they ordered a new pair well in advance, in the summer, so as to give the leather time to harden before the testing winter set in. Old boots, well-worn, served well for wear at harvest time; the rents between uppers and soles only helped to cool feet that often ached on the sun-burned stubble.

Everyone looked to harvest earnings for the extra money for new boots for the family. And the bootmaker knew this and worked to it; the many pairs he made in advance (on that understanding) were a very important part of his livelihood. The village feast fell at a lucky time for all concerned — just on the edge of winter, when back money, due on harvest earnings, had been paid. Gladly mixing business with pleasure, they all assembled at the bootmaker's house to supper, where they feasted together to the honour of the boots that he had made.

The Saddler

The saddlers' trade was with those who kept horses; the farmers, therefore, were his best customers. Their workshops likewise smelt of wax and leather, but their method of work differed from the bootmaker's: the saddlers were even greater experts at stitching with the awl and waxed threads; the traces that took the strong pull of the horse on the wagon were made of a thickness of two or three strips of leather united by many rows of hand-stitching.

The saddlers' work varied from the large harness for plough horses to the light equipment of the quick-trotting pony. Horse collars from farms were often brought to be relined and stuffed, the leather seared by the sun, wind, and rains of the open fields.

On those fields mere appearance was not of importance; but every well-managed farm had its complete sets of harness in good condition for travel beyond the farm, to and from market or station. Then the well-matched horses, sleek with health and attention, were the special pride of both farmer and carter; and their good points were enhanced by harness rich with shining brass buckles, and with ornaments on which the initials of the owner were chased. It enhanced their value (it certainly aided a sale when, as often happened, the farmer was open to sell them). The horses so harnessed to a well-painted wagon were called a *good turn-out*. A good turn-out suggested a well-stocked and well-managed farm, and a substantial balance at the bank.

Of course the harness-makers played up to this good spirit. They hung long-handled whips on the wall outside their shop — whips with dark woven jackets, ringed from end to end with ferrules of shining brass of diminishing size. There they temptingly caught the eyes of ploughboys and carters bringing harness to be mended. It was naught but a matter of tact, of catching the master in a generous mood, of suggesting the need and advantage, not for whipping but for appearance, and just to let the horses know that they *had* one in their hand. The harness-maker understood his craft, and he knew how to make the best of the carters' pride in their horses.

Thatchers

Thatching was a separate craft that had not changed, when I first knew of it, in either materials or method. The straw still came from wheat grown in the parish, and was laid on the roofs according to strictly unchanged traditional practices. But the quality of the straw was not so good as formerly, for the threshing machine damaged it. Old Enoch often said that when corn was threshed by flails a good coat of thatch lasted twenty years, whereas with machine-threshed straw it would only last ten. He also said that to save the straw from being broken by the flails the ears of corn were often chopped off and threshed separately. He worked regularly for my father and was a knowing old man, with a memory that carried back many long years before I was born. His yarns were often so tall that it asked an effort to believe them, but at least I never had reason to doubt what he said about thatching.

The thatchers worked in pairs, the master on the roof laying the straw in place, and his assistant preparing the *yolms* and carrying them up the ladder for use. The yolms were small bundles of straws, each straight and in order: the assistant prepared them by pulling handfuls from a pile; the pulling action caused them to be parallel. The thatchers' system was to lay a strip as wide as could be reached to the right side of the ladder, extending from eaves to ridge. This they called a *stulch*. At both eaves

69

and ridge, also at hips, barges and gables, in fact, at any projection of the roof liable to damage by gales, they fastened the thatch down with cleft willow or hazel sprays. These not only secured it, but also gave what seems essential to all craft work — an effective finish.

The thought of beauty is seldom absent from the mind of a worker, whatever his craft may be. Mind and hands, working together, may indeed make what is strictly and simply useful, but if it is nothing more, then the spirit remains unsatisfied. There is in man an urge that demands expression, a desire that the finished work shall not only serve its purpose, but that it shall also have about it some quality that gives pleasure. And the banding of thatched roofs is as good an illustration of this principle as any other; the simple, cleft willow bands, fastened to the smooth expanses of thatch in parallel-spaced lines, with zigzag or crossed bands between, are like embroidery in their effect. The thatchers were (and still are) a homely folk who make no pretence to art; yet their work has its own characteristic beauty.

Brewing

The village formerly brewed its own beer; and its beer was so good, it seems, that a barrel was carved in a bench end at the church, though no one knows if it was done out of honour to the cooper who made it or to the man who filled it afterwards. Every farm had its large brewing copper in which the malt and hops were boiled; the liquid from the first brew was known as *best* and that from the second as *small beer*. Beer was the drink of all; the *best* for the house, and special occasions, and the *small* for general use on the farm. So it had been in the days of the fathers, and so it seemed to many it should continue for all time.

The farmers used their own barley, but bought the hops. The barley was taken to the maltsters to be soaked and turned and re-turned until it sprouted; and was then dried in the maltsters' kiln. The preparation of so much malt meant work for a good many people and the malt-kiln roof, four-sided with a louver at top, was a feature of almost all villages.

The malthouse was a long building of two floors, each of them being faced with concrete. At one end of the lower floor was a pump and a concrete tank where the barley was soaked. After soaking it was shovelled out on to the concrete floor and turned daily, the turning being always in one direction, so that each day the heap travelled one stage farther along the long floor. This enabled the maltster to treat the barley of others at the same time, one lot following the other. On reaching the end of the lower floor it was thrown on to the floor above, which, for that reason, did not reach quite to the end of the building. The turning was repeated daily along the top floor until the sprouted barley finally reached the other end, where a door opened on to the floor of the kiln.

The kiln was a square brick structure with a four-hipped and tiled roof surmounted by a wooden louver through which the fumes and steam escaped. Its floor was of red clay tiles, each ten inches square by one and a half inches thick; these rested on strong iron rods built into the walls at each side. The making of these tiles was itself a little triumph of the clay-workers' art; each was pitted for two-thirds of its thickness by no fewer than 137 three-quarter inch holes, and then, at the butt end of each of these holes, seven minute holes, each a little over one-sixteenth of an inch, were pierced, every hole remaining clear and true after the whole tile was burned.

These tiles, laid edge to edge with the small holes uppermost, formed a level floor through which the heat could percolate in equal strength all over its area; the sprouted barley was spread upon it, where it was dried by the heat ascending from a furnace beneath. The heat changed the barley to malt, which, for beer, was roasted to a nut-brown, but for stout or porter, to a deeper colour.

Besides malting for other people, the maltsters formerly also sold their own prepared malt. An old account book records sales in the year 1740 at 3s. 8d. per bushel. In the year 1742, the price was 3s. 6d., and in 1744 and 1745 it had dropped to 2s. 8d.

As a side-line to his regular business, about a century later than this, one maltster of our village extracted teeth. One of father's joiners, when a boy, had a tooth drawn; he said that the maltster laid him on a stone flag floor and, kneeling on his chest, pinched the hollow double tooth until it split; he then pulled out the fragments singly.

One maltster of the village also owned a complete brewery where we often had carpentry to do. I loved to explore those buildings (the doors of which bore strange inscriptions) where huge dark vats of oak reposed. Unlike the flour mills that we also repaired, or my father's workshop, there was no dust or litter of shavings; the aroma, too, was entirely different, at times it was the smell of scalded hops, or *grains* (malt after brewing), all reeking hot from the copper. As I did not like the taste of beer I never drank it, though father's men spared no words in its praise; but I liked the brewery nevertheless.

Once when I was a youth we helped a cooper put together an enormous vat in the basement. I was put inside with a lighted candle, and told to guide the top and base of the vat into the grooves of the staves, while the workers outside put on the broad iron bands and hammered them tight. When all was properly together, a small square was cut out of the top to let me out, the men reaching down to haul me up. This was much to the relief of the brewer's wife, who all the time had anxiously inquired, through the walls of my airtight prison, if I was feeling all right.

Tailors

There were also those of the village who made clothing for the men and women; male tailors who sat cross-legged on benches, hand-stitching "leather-cloth" and corduroy, for so long that one wondered if their legs would ever have power to resume a leg's proper action. It seemed to me a job for which man was not intended; I never envied them, nor did I ever learn anything about their methods of work.

Yet I, of course, like all the rest, had to go to them when need was. They and their customers were necessarily in frequent contact, whether it was a matter of breeches for the farmer who rode to hounds, or heavy cord trousers and sleeve waistcoats for the labourer of the bleak open fields, it had to be discussed in person. Only reliable workmanship could stand against the strong tide of local opinion, always voiced freely, for or against. But a satisfied customer never budged from the tailor who had served him well in cloth and price.

They changed not their styles to please passing fashions, and continued to make on the same lines for so long as I could remember. By certain peculiarities of cut and fit it was not difficult to know a villager's tailor. One of ours employed assistants, and himself regularly attended market, to get orders from farmers. Another tailor of ours studied human ailments, as a side-line, and brewed raw quinine, which once bucked me up when I was feeling limp. He was also good at sealing wounds with plaster, which he cut into narrow strips and placed crosswise over the injury. To make the plaster stick he heated the ends of the strips on his flat-iron. The village had cause to value his services, for at that time it had no resident doctor, or trained ambulance men.

Then, as now, the women were more independent of aid in their personal attire. When dressmakers were wanted they usually attended at the homes; there the cutting, fitting, and stitching went on, interspersed with lively chatter. Rarely did unappreciative man come into contact with this element of life; not for his benefit was the chance remark that a "fullness wanted taking in", or that another part needed letting out. His absence, at those times, was usually better liked than his company.

A few dressmakers, however, maintained establishments of their own, where all was done to beautify further a sex naturally beautiful.

Lace-making

The lovely craft of making lace by hand, with bobbins on a pillow, was an industry that expired, as such, about the time of my early life; though lace was still made for private customers by elderly women of the village, whose lives and habits seemed as beautiful as the creations that left their hands.

To me, as to other outsiders, the method was a mystery; yet to those dames it seemed to be simplicity itself, a mere adjustment of pins on the pattern, with a curious jingling throw of the bobbins one over the other, followed by another pin adjustment, and so on. The watcher knew that the work was going forward, but the advance was almost imperceptibly slow. Undoubtedly it was love for the craft that kept them at it, not the little money earned by so many hours of devoted labour.

Each dame knew herself to be one of few lace-makers left, though they all remembered the time when the knowledge had been so general that schools for training were regularly held; but now nearly all who had followed the craft had died and left it to them, and the demand had dwindled until it was not worth while for others to learn it. For those that still made lace in my time, it seemed to be reward enough when lovers of the beautiful bent over the pillow and examined the delicacy of the work, for then they knew the joy that is always felt when two kindred loves fuse in a common object.

In the heyday of lace-making my father's younger brother had turned bobbins by the score for the workers of the village, the demand for them being once swiftly increased by a change of fashion which needed them of heavier make. Once only I tried my hand at it when a lady wanted some bobbins turned from the wood of a favourite walnut tree. I found the task difficult for my tools; our lathes were far too cumbersome for so delicate a job, and the speed was far too slow.

The Millers

The village had its mills, both wind and water driven. They were part of its original self-sustaining completeness, survivals of the time when each community catered for itself and no other.

The milling of corn, both imported and home-grown, was still a thriving trade when I was a boy. A mill gave its owner then an assured position in the district, and so it seemed likely to continue for all time. A fall in the price of corn was no calamity to millers, for it enabled them to purchase cheaply; they therefore thrived when farmers found conditions difficult.

Village life without its mills was unthinkable; they were integral to the life of both farm and cottage. Although the bakers were their largest customers for flour, many villagers, including my own parents, still bought it by the bushel or sack and made their own bread, which they baked in the large brick oven that was to be found in almost every substantial house. The miller also catered for the livestock on the farms, and the cottager's pig, ducks, and fowls.

The practice of milling had much the character of a craft; indeed the dressing of the grinding face of mill stones was a highly skilled operation, and only perfectly dressed stones could produce finely ground flour or meals.

The methods of dressing the stones, and the methods of grinding, were much the same in both types of mills, though the structures and position of water-mills and windmills were necessarily very different. The water-mill had to be near a stream where a good fall of water could be harnessed, but a windmill might be erected in any position where a good head of wind blew. The water-mill of the village is a mile away, but the windmills were close at hand. The structures of the two kinds of mills, too, were entirely different, the water-mill being built of brick and stone, for it never needed to be moved, whereas the windmill was of wood, cleverly built, and designed so that it could be turned to face the wind from any quarter. How important wind was to country people in those days may be known by recalling that a long-continued calm sent up the price of bread.

Our repairs to the carpentry of mills enabled us to become familiar with the construction and machinery of both types. The skeleton timbers of the windmill were so strong that they never needed repairs. But we often repaired the outside boarding of the walls; and from time to time we inserted new wooden cogs to the wheels, as we did for the mills driven by water. This was a dusty yet interesting job, one that needed great accuracy, involving mechanical principles that (we realized) were laid down, learned, and followed centuries earlier when the mills were first made. Windmill or water-mill in action was a pleasant sound to hear: the rhythmical rumble of huge wheels and heavy revolving stones, together with the merry "click, click" of the steel shaker that regulated the flow of corn to the stones; but the grandeur and roar of the windmill sails was of a majesty that could not be surpassed. Of all the memorable places where our work took us, none was quite so good as the mills.

Bakers

The bakers who converted the millers' flour into good bread were a busy folk who rose early and worked late. The excellence of the crisp, crusty bread that they made from that stone-ground flour gives them the right to a craftsman's dignity too. They made it into quartern and half-quartern loaves, golden and russet brown. The crust crackled between the teeth. The crust at the bottom of the loaf had ridges made by the joints of the tiles in the oven. Their baking was done in brick-built, domed ovens with floors of square twelve-inch tiles. These ovens were heated either by a furnace at an angle, or by faggots of wood that blazed in the inside of the oven itself until the bricks became hot. When the oven was well heated, the baker carefully wiped the floor down with a damp rag fixed to a long pole called a *mawker*.

The baking of such ovens was perfect: one uniform radiation of heat that seemed to infuse the bread with sweetness.

They had no inspector to fear, so it did not trouble them if, by baking those loaves thoroughly, the weight was reduced. They did not deliver their loaves from door to door (at least until shortly before the date of my birth). Many villagers still baked their own bread every week, and had recourse to the shop only when the home supply was short. The home-made loaf of those days did not become uneatable if kept a week; it was said to have good staying properties on which hard work could be done.

The masoners of the village built the ovens from special bricks that would withstand heat. Bricks retain warmth for a long time; thus once those ovens were heated they never afterwards became cold. Sometimes tiles of the floor became loose and hindered the baker's wooden peel as he passed the loaves inside. Then a masoner, Alfred Chapman, was sent for to creep in and put them right. The work was dangerous, for the heat was intense and the oven so shallow that he was obliged to work lying on his chest. Once his assistant had heard him call faintly for help, and dragged him out in the nick of time, quite exhausted.

The Village Stores

With so many useful tradesmen and craftsmen the old village society was able in large measure to cater for everybody's needs. They all had contra accounts with one another, and so little trade went on with neighbouring towns that one carrier with a donkey cart was able to do it all, and even he, it was understood, went to town weekly only if he had orders enough to make the journey worth while. In consequence, the village stores prospered.

The principal store was called *The Beehive*. A straw-woven hive was hung for a sign over its door. Another was known as *The Tea-caddy*; and a third, which baked bread as well, was called *The Wheatsheaf.*

The Beehive was certainly busy: hogsheads of moist sugar and large loaves of hard white sugar might be seen arriving — the moist to be weighed and sold by the pound; the white, before sale, to be broken and afterwards chopped with an implement worked by a lad at the end of the counter. He was supposed to chop into sizes convenient for the teacup, yet many found it wise to keep their own small *sugar nipper* on the tea table to break the larger lumps. I envied that boy his job, chopping for hours on end, in the midst of sweetness.

The whole village seemed to converge upon the Beehive, and it would be difficult to mention a need that it did not supply. A large green canister of dark treacle stood on the counter. It had an iron handle at the bottom, which opened and closed a hole through which the syrup ran out. We fetched it away in our own earthenware jars; it was sold by the pound; and the grocers were skilful in managing the valve so as to cut off the flow at exactly the right weight. The young assistant would furtively pass his fingers through the treacle stream as the flow diminished and so to his mouth. A finger of mine would likewise find its way into the jar before I got home.

Ponderous cheeses rested on a back counter, into which, when their quality was questioned by a customer, the proprietor passed a "taster" — a steel implement, small and tapered, like an auger in curve. With this he neatly withdrew a small cube of cheese; the client broke a piece from the end and ate it, and the cube was passed back into its original place, which it fitted exactly.

On a high shelf large tin canisters of tea were ranged side by side, each with Chinese symbols painted in rich colours on the front. Much handling had given those canisters a look of great and venerable age; they looked as if they held the occult blends for which the store was famous; for the flavour of the tea that the ladies drank had no small part in maintaining the Beehive's popularity.

Half-way down the store, where two posts supported the floor above, the grocery ended and the drapery began. There, one suddenly noticed an entirely different atmosphere — not food, now, but clothes prevailed; and the decorum, too, was different; customer and assistant were more sedate; by comparison, in the grocery, their ways appeared altogether more rough and ready.

In the grocery department the counters were built of pine, seared and white with incessant cleaning; here they were made of wide Spanish mahogany, mellow with long usage. Bales of drapery were stacked on shelves on both sides; and rolls of "coco-matting" and linoleum stood on end at an angle to the counter. These, with a hundred and one other smaller items, together filled that part of the store with its own particular aroma, highly characteristic and quite different from anything anywhere else in the village.

Ironmongery, benzoline and paraffin, lamps and candles seemed to be a secondary line, yet of importance. Though included in the grocery department, these were discreetly kept separate from all the eatables. Somewhere at the back was a store, unrevealed to customers, to which continual resort was made. There the greaves were stocked in slabs the size of small gravestones. These were made of the residue of the tallow-chandler, dried skins and glutinous shreds from which the fat had been squeezed. The cottagers bought them for fattening the ducks for the London market.

CHAPTER
FIVE

Gnawing it Out

A large part of the trade within the village was carried on by a system called *gnawing it out* — a method something like the primitive trade by barter in days before coin came into general use.

As far as can be ascertained, the name came from the former practice on some farms, where the labourers were expected to take milk, potatoes, or a joint of pork or mutton, as part of their wages. They dubbed this *gnawing it out*, and so it is believed it came to be adopted by tradesmen.

The butcher, having had his cart repaired by the wheelwright, rather than part with ready cash, expected the wheelwright to run up a bill for meat in settlement. The system worked both ways, the wheelwright often being of like mind and motive. It was more or less the same in almost all the other trades; each individual thus secured to himself an assured amount of custom, and the whole village kept its trade to its own circle.

The boy at the village school was taught that the debtor was servant to the creditor. But on leaving school, if he should happen eventually to take up trade in the village, he found the principle reversed. He learned that coin was a cherished commodity, highly prized and far from plentiful, and that many who were known to have it were as likely as those who had none to plead inability to pay the amount they owed him. Having rendered his account for work done or goods supplied, he found it next to impossible to get the money. In despair he had at last to fall into line with the time-honoured method of taking, instead of money, the particular commodity that the debtor was able to supply. Nor would it be long before he discovered that by rendering his own account he had placed himself at the debtor's mercy: once the debtor knew exactly the amount he owed he was certain to hold his own contra statement back at least until that debt was cleared; or even worse, when the long-deferred settlement did at last take place, the creditor might find that instead of taking some money he had some to pay.

To draw the balance at settlement was the studied ambition of many. As, however, everyone could not do this, those who knew the amount of their own indebtedness were at an advantage. This was easy enough when trading with one like my father, who always rendered his accounts quarterly and, if they were not paid, sent the "account rendered" at the appointed times. I am quite sure that the cute ones were amused at his simple straightforwardness, and that — although the reminders may have been irritating — they were glad to know just what they owed him; it was a simple matter then to compare the amount with the total standing against him in their own ledgers, biding the time when it should be more than their own debt. Father knew this full well yet he never departed from his system.

The matter was very different when both parties were of the same disposition, acting with the same motive, and knowing the dodge to the last letter. Then it was "diamond cut diamond" indeed, fruitless attempts on each side to get a bill from the other; each determined not to be the first to declare, because each knew for certain that the other would straightway make his to a larger sum. And so these contra transactions often went on for years without any account being rendered, each year making the settlement more difficult. One that I knew about was finally squared, *after fourteen years*, by tossing for a sovereign between them.

The method of semi-barter called *chop* was also popular. To take some animal or article in part payment and to draw cash for the balance was an ideal transaction to many. It was once explained to me that the chop system secured double advantages, a profit on the sale and on whatever was taken in exchange; and further, that when making the chop you had only to assure yourself that it was for something of greater value, and you might pleasantly dream of beginning with a donkey, changing it for a pony, and end up as the proud possessor of a blood horse!

It was noticeable that those who favoured these principles usually had money, however careful they might be to keep the knowledge of it from others. The policy of always *drawing* on a deal and rarely, if ever, paying out, could not fail to fill that pocket which, for safety, rather than convenience, was at the back of the trousers behind the hip. There, where no intruding hand could reach, safe within its strong lining, was the strong

hessian purse, like a miniature sack with two compartments, one for silver and the other for gold, the shillings,
florins, and half-crowns, the sovereigns and halves all
warming together; pressure on the flesh there gave
assurance to the spirit; it was felt as a constant
companion, a perpetual monitor, urging to go one better
than before.

The village seemed the embodiment of peace, an
outward expression of guileless life. The thatch of its
cottages embraced their lattice windows; the flowers of
the gardens, the very moss and lichens, all combined to
suggest carefree repose. The villagers themselves, with
their homely garb and quaint speech, innocently gave an
impression of simple life and ideals. Yet often their
wariness could not be surpassed.

The thrift of many generations had been handicapped
by too narrow a scope; each had lived, more or less, on
the others, the land around forming the single basis of all
their livelihoods. They knew each other's mentalities,
habits and ways only too well. And when two equally
wary ones set out to deal, the deal became a battle of
wits, with each man doing his best to come out on the
sunny side.

Banks, of course, were altogether distrusted. They
might break, as some had done; and, what was as bad,
those in charge would know just how much money one
had. The post office was managed by one of themselves,
which made the risk to any secret even greater. Far
better, they held, to keep the cash one had where it
would be at hand if wanted. The policy demanded very
cautious conduct: the pose of poverty had to be

maintained by avoidance of pretentious dress or any other outward display. But the drab attire was mentally contrasted with the well-filled purse; its meanness was suffused with the lustre of virtue; they prided themselves on appearing poor.

But their fellow-villagers were rarely deceived. Life was far too intimate. They were bound to observe and note every source of income and expenditure; they knew to a certainty who was saving money and who was not. Only, as they did not know for certain the actual amount, it naturally became magnified in imagination. Of one man they said that for many years past he had saved every sixpenny piece that came into his hands; it was a principle with him, they said, and he would not depart from it for any inconvenience it might cause him. More than this, the number of sixpences so saved, said rumour, had increased until they filled a peck measure, and he now and then amused himself by counting them, building little tiers of coins, like the picture of a miser. The "stocking up the chimney", though not necessarily literal, was understood by all; it suggested wealth secretly hoarded.

Village life was too narrow for such attributions not to reach the owner's ears. Remarks, jocularly made, began to look sinister when too much meditated upon; the mind became obsessed with dreadful doubts. Robbery was not unknown; who knew what might happen at home? One man, they said, drew two buckets of water from the well every night and stood them just inside the door to welcome any intruder. Another balanced his biggest tray insecurely so that the noise as it fell should frighten whoever upset it.

CHAPTER SIX

The Cottager's Pig

The miller had many customers in the village, for almost all the cottagers kept their pig and had to go to him for pig food. Even the thrifty folk — those who grew barley on their allotments to fatten it with — were dependent on the miller to grind it into meal. He had an easy way of doing business and attended at the *Red Lion* every Friday evening. There, after the day's work was done, the pig-keepers called, also those who bred ducks, called "duckers". There the sack of toppings or barley meal on account was paid for and another ordered; the transaction was made genial by the pint of mild they drank to his health and prosperity.

Life without a pig was almost unthinkable. To have a sty in the garden, or, as often, abutting on the cottage, was held to be as essential to the happiness of a newly married couple as a living room or a bedroom. So much was the pig a part of domestic life that no vision was satisfactory that did not include the flitch of bacon on the wall of the living room, and hams and gammons hanging from the ceiling.

The more substantial cottager, midway between the labourer and farmer, kept his breeding sow, and a happy man he was when it responded to wise pre-arrangements and farrowed in the early spring. The news that a litter of (say) ten or twelve sucklings had arrived in the night never failed to create a sensation in the placid life of the village. Cautious peeps over the rude sty fence were allowed, for a glimpse of the happy mother lying flat-wise on a bed of clean straw, her sleek black youngsters sleeping, or, as often, securing a teat of luscious milk. The smallest, the last to be born, was called the *dillen*, a local term that was also applied to the undersized chick or duckling in a brood. If the sow gave birth to a litter beyond the number of teats that she had, the dillen was taken away to be weaned by hand. The little pig, so favoured, often had its first habitation in a cosy basket or box on the floor of the ingle nook indoors, where, on a soft bed of hay or straw, it slept away the times between its meals from the bottle.

When the family of little pigs was eight to ten weeks' old, the bliss of life in the parental sty was disturbed. In the evenings, after the day's work was done, one by one the cottagers arrived, sack in hand. After much haggling and bargaining, a purchase was almost certain to be made. The chosen pig suddenly found itself caught by a hind leg, and, in spite of its shrill squeals and the deep-throated protests of its mother, found itself at last inside the sack. There, to its relief, was a proviso of safety against suffocation, arranged beforehand by the cottager — a hole, big enough for its little snout, but not big enough for its little head.

It was a familiar sight to see a pig being carried like this, the villager walking along, sack over shoulder, with a little pig's nose protruding from a hole in the sack.

The little pig whose fortune it was to have a cottage home, henceforward was definitely "in clover". An extra warm bed had been carefully prepared for its first few days away from mother, and afterwards, from the hour when it was safely installed in its sty, never for a moment was its welfare absent from the minds of husband and wife. To feed it, to clean out the sty, to shake up its bed and add clean straw when it was wanted, were duties never forgotten. Their pig was a liability which would in due course swallow up more than half the husband's earnings. They knew this, and had to plan ahead so that, by the exercise of stringent economy, they might meet the ever-increasing cost of its food. That liability was sometimes eased a bit by a knowledge of the potatoes and barley that would be obtained from the allotment by and by, when the little pig was big. The waste from the garden, trimmings of cabbages, peelings from potatoes and turnips, all and sundry, were put by for its meals. The stock-pot — usually an old iron boiler — was given a special place over the home fire, and all the scraps went into this, where they simmered and melted to a pulpy mass called *todge*. Todge had a far-reaching smell, a smell that seemed definitely related to the pig cult.

The lore and cult of the pig formed a bond between the villagers, as strong as if it had been inherited. All understood it naturally, save, maybe, the Parson. He, poor man, fresh, from college, could not be expected to know more than which was the head and which the tail. They pitied his ignorance; yet should a cottager have the misfortune to lose a pig through illness, they relied on him to draw up (and head) an appeal for contributions, to which they were all ready to subscribe.

To call on a neighbour without asking "How's the pig a-doing?" was a plain breach of courtesy, not to be lightly excused. The walk round the garden on a Sunday, or of an evening, the detailed examination of the growing cabbages, the savoys, the sprouts, the beans and the peas, would have seemed incomplete without a long and interested pause at the sty, and a learned discussion on the merits of the particular pig.

Sties were often ramshackle and remarkable; rude lean-to roofs of sticks and straw, heaped and thatched, generally leaning against the solid wall of the cottage, or of an outhouse. The complete sty comprised covered sleeping quarters with a fenced-in yard in front. The floor to both was formed with rough stones rammed tight edgewise, side by side. My father sold the thick slabs sawn from the outside of elm butts for the walls of sties. The men came with wheelbarrows to buy them; they called them *slabbin*. Their outer sides were convex, and the edges crooked. It would have been difficult even for a good carpenter to make airtight walls with them. But experience proved that the flow of fresh air afforded by faulty joints was good for the pig. Those farmers, butchers, and tradesfolk, who were able to afford neat brick sties, with tiled or slated roofs, and floors paved with bricks or cement, found that in course of time their pigs did not thrive anything like so well. The cottager's pig in its crazy sty was far happier; it lay and slept contentedly or grunted and fed, and never ceased meantime to put on size, flesh, and fat.

The art of pig-keeping was by no means so simple as it seemed. To feed a young pig on rich food would make it fat internally and retard its growth. Little and often — sweet toppings, fresh from the mill, stirred to thick gruel with greasy wash from the house — this was the policy first adopted. It had to be given in a shallow small-size trough — feeding the little pig from a large deep trough would have developed a permanent hunch on its back. The wise man kept it growing naturally until of mature size; *then* the food was given in quantity and quality, for the definite object of fattening, called *finishing it off*.

The principle of giving no more food than could be eaten straightaway was strictly adhered to. To see that it had been licked up to the last drop was proof that the pig was thriving. It gave the owner joy to see that the trough, if it was a wooden one, had its grain raised and polished by the tongue, or, if it was iron, that it was left dark and glistening. These signs showed a happy pig, with a good appetite, and were always accompanied by steadily continued increase in size. Pure greediness was a virtue; a pig's desire to eat and sleep showed that it was "a-doing".

The little pig soon grew used to the routine of the cottage life; there, peering through the chinks of its prison, it learned to know its owner's times — time to go to work and time to come home. Had he a titbit in his hand or pocket? Some oddment picked up on the wayside, a few windfall apples, or acorns, or the leaf of a cabbage to fling over, to eat or to play with? Pig knew full well that Man would never pass Sty without a pause and a glance within; that often indeed he would bend over the fence and lovingly scratch along the spine and behind the ears — parts so difficult to rub — the act that gave indescribable pleasure!

To the pig, the owner was a god, the supreme being controlling all the events of its life. Before he went off to work in the early morning, he brought delicious food to the sty — sweet meal, stirred with "todge" from the stockpot, and flavoured with the greasy wash from dinner plates and dishes, pudding cloths and saucepans. He it was who repeated the service at mid-day and evening; who carefully cleaned the sty yard and renewed the handful of small coal or cinders to crunch, and thus stimulated the flow of saliva so essential to good digestion. In short, the pig's whole happiness, through-out its brief life, was dependent on its owner's labour.

It is said — with truth — that pigs have a marvellous sense of hearing. Throughout the fair mornings of summer, while the early dew still sparkled in the advancing sunlight, the pig would listen for the sound of the opening cottage door and the rattle of the bucket into which its morning meal was being stirred. Then squealings would begin, ravenous impatience at necessary delay, vigorous shovings and shakings with its snout at the fastened sty gate, or now and then, standing on hind-legs with fore-feet at the fence, fringed, anxious eyes looking to the top over which the visage of the owner would soon appear. His hand would carry the precious food; and his problem would then be how to defeat the pig's eager attempts to grab it from the bucket, and how to pour it safely into the trough.

When you have two or more pigs together in a sty, they will gobble the food with the utmost speed, each anxious to get down as much as possible before the other can eat it. But the cottager's pig, with a sty to itself, was subject to no such fear. Once the waiting time was over and the food safely in the trough, its gratified manner of feeding — the delighted "suck, suck", of the mealy liquid — was a pleasure to watch. It really did the owner good to see the pig eat, and eat, as though its whole disposition conspired only to that end. Its back was daily becoming longer and broader; hidden away under the glossy black hair, lay prospective hams, gammons, chines, haseletts, and rearings, not to mention the two flitches of streaky bacon that, later on, would grace the wall of his living room. His heart warmed with genial tolerance; it was good policy to be generous and kind.

Into the serene life of the pig, the otherwise perpetual bliss that covered a spring, summer, and autumn, there came one experience of deep humiliation, one drastic curb to its own self-gratification. Grateful indeed it was for the good food so regularly supplied, yet it had no corresponding respect for the sty in which it was so comfortably housed. Let but its stomach be filled and the pangs of hunger appeased, its mind sought recreation. The heavy iron trough afforded a delightful plaything; this it would gaily turn over and over with its strong snout, or lift one end and let it fall with a resounding bang on the hard stone floor. In a pig's defence we admit that its natural order of life would have been an open field in which it would have roamed and routed at will, and that, in comparison, the sty was a cramped and narrow existence. As a youngster it was content with a scamper into the dim recesses of the sleeping quarters, from whence to reappear at the doorway with a defiant grunt; also to use the carefully spread litter as a routing ground, which it ploughed into furrows with its little snout, and left in a condition of chaos. But a grown pig needed more substantial pleasures. This was afforded by the cobble stones that paved the floor. The investigating snout probed round about until a stone that could be moved was found, with the result that, on the return of the cottager, he found half the floor heaved up and the whole sty in disorder. One remedy only was available, "to have the pig rung as soon as possible".

And here, from beyond sixty vanished years, a personal experience re-arises. Three boys, myself the second in age, are at their mother's side, she with her baby in her lap. It was the short period of relaxation and homely chat after tea. An unknown man passed the window, heading towards the pigsty in our orchard. "He is going to ring the pig", said my elder brother, knowingly. Without the least idea of what would happen, I ran to the sty and, unseen by the man who had entered the enclosure, peered through a chink of the fence. I saw him noose a pig by the nose with a cord and pull it to a post to which he tied it. Shrieks rent the air, noises so piercing, so heartrending that, crying, I fled in terror to bury my face in my mother's lap.

Ringing the village pigs was a side-line of the blacksmith's business, probably because he had the horse-shoe nails of which the rings were made. Two rings, one to each nostril, were inserted. By noosing the pig's upper jaw behind the large fangs, and tying the cord to a post, one man did the ringing singlehanded. He prepared the rings beforehand, curving each nail with its ends left open wide enough to pass over the thick extrusion at the end of the snout. The pig was so alarmed, and so anxious to regain freedom, that I doubt if it realized what was taking place; the pain it felt could not have been anything like as bad as the noise it made. Its sustained pull backwards at the cord brought the snout into an ideal position. A quick push passed the curved nail through the thin skin, one to each nostril. A pinch with the pliers closed each ring, and the discomfited pig was released. Only a tinge of blood appeared and in a very short time the snout seemed to accommodate itself to them. Throughout the day, however, the pig slept away the effects of its agitating experience.

The joys of routing thus ended, nothing remained but surrender to the blisses of eating and sleeping. To grow fast, and grow fat, made exertion less and less desirable. What need for effort with life so bountifully full? To sleep the sleep of the just was better — with eyes slightly open — emitting melodious snores — and so to wile away the sultry hours of summer; to stretch the long body at ease on the soft straw in the cool shade of the shed, head only at the doorway to sniff the fragrant air from off the cottage garden and the valley beyond. This was the life of the pig.

Now and then it visited its favourite rubbing post, generally the weakest of all that held the fence in position. Other posts offered equal consolation, but it declined to use them. The chosen post was worn smooth and shiny by the strenuous pushes of its strong chine; the fence would lean till it was in danger of collapse, and a series of struts had to be added to keep it up. Such perversity constituted the humour of pig cult; it consoled the owner as he laboured to keep the fence from falling down.

And the time was near, he knew, when relationship would be reversed. The days were shortening; already a nip — the foretaste of winter — was in the early morning air, and crimsoned leaves fell, fluttering, from the trees. Summer was giving place to winter; the time to transfer the pig from the sty to the cottage was close at hand.

Perhaps every owner, when moralizing, felt himself a traitor to the animal he had so carefully tended; knowing the tragic end that neared, he was glad of the pig's ignorance. Memory of personal sacrifices gave him further consolation: the daily denials made necessary by the enormous amount of food that the pig had eaten; the extra hours of work on the garden and allotment in producing the potatoes and barley for its food, all hard labour, all freely rendered. Looking at it from that angle he was able to call it a square deal, a realization of invested capital, with interest.

We draw a veil over the act of killing, and ease our minds with the knowledge that more humane methods are now adopted. Dispositions then, as now, were plastic and conformed to the inevitable, but everyone, I believe, was glad when it was over. As children we remained indoors for the worst, and sallied forth to see the pig lying dead on a thin layer of clean wheat straw, with the butcher carefully shaking straws all over its glossy back and tucking wisps between its legs. It looked quite happy. The burning was a part of the ritual that we were always keen to see. We loved to hear the crackling of the blazing straw and to watch the flames leap and chase each other high in the air and to smell the smell of singed hair mingled with the scent of burning straw.

It was a rite of age-long distinction. As Druids round a sacrificial fire, so ranged the group around that blazing pyre. The butcher stood venerable in his long smock frock; as a bishop held his crozier, so he handled his long fork. Within the golden ring of light he seemed to be the high priest of a pagan ceremony, his dress and fork the symbols of his office. As the blaze died down he turned the pig over and covered it with straw as before; then with his fork he passed a wisp of straw that had been kept alight to the pyre, and the fire blazed again. The swirling flames leapt and danced, lights flashing and changing in the gathering shades of evening.

Two main burnings were necessary; and usually two smaller burnings followed. As the pig lay on its side, the hairs from the back and belly were not all burnt away. These needed turning upward; small quantities of straw were burned to get rid of them. Finally, a strong broom was applied with vigour to the carcase, to sweep away the smut and residue of burnt hair and straw. Then the "pig ladder", like a rude ambulance, was brought, and the carcase was turned on to it and carried to a place convenient for washing. Buckets of water were thrown on its steaming sides, while the butcher deftly scraped the skin from head to tail. Then the pig changed completely. It was no longer the black pig that we remembered so well in the sty, but became a hairless mottled brown carcase.

I was always surprised at the ease with which the butcher pulled off the horns from the toes. As he threw them away, boys, looking on, chased after them; they were warm from the fire, with cup-like interiors that interested us. Boys who lived hard gnawed the tender ends and seemed to enjoy them. The butcher then made a deft cut to the middle joint of each leg and turned each hock backward. The carcase was ready for opening and removal of the offals.

He knew the anatomy of a pig; his cuts were quick and decisive. The multitude of organs — entrails, liver, lights, heart, and tongue — were all skilfully separated and removed. The bladder was drained and blown out to its full size, the shape of a Rugger ball. It needed strong lungs, the stem broken from a clay pipe, and an extra pair of hands, ready with string to tie it quickly before the wind escaped. In days before pots were plentiful the bladders were filled with lard, poured in hot through a funnel. My mother used the skin of the bladder for covering home-made preserves.

The killing of the pig was the great event in the domestic life of the year. All other duties were held over for it. No woman was ever heard to complain of the work it involved. It was accepted as a challenge, a decisive test of her position in the village as a capable wife. Certainly mothers expected to help the newly married daughters with their first pig, and would have felt hurt if they had not been asked to do so. Neighbours, too, were equally interested and ready to lend a hand with the cutting up of the *flear*, the making of the lard, and the hundred and one other jobs that fell to the lot of the wife. No ordinary household could have eaten all the offal from a pig, therefore much was disposed of. The liver was usually sold in advance, also the *haseletts* — prime joints of lean pork, cut near the backbone. The period of pig-killing was a bad time for the local butchers; trade was slow and they were glad when the season had passed.

A fatty smell, readily recognized by a caller, pervaded the whole house while lard-making was going forward. If the weight of the flear in pounds equalled the scores of the carcase it proved that the pig had been correctly fatted. In my home the first dish to appear on the table was the residue from the lard, toasted crisp. We called them *critlings*. I was never fond of them, nor of chitterlings, though many spared not words in their praise. My thoughts were in advance, dwelling on the delicacies that I knew would follow.

The offals removed, the carcase was carried to a cool outhouse, where the flesh became cold and solid. It was hung by the jaw on a large spike that had been driven into a beam for that purpose years before; many pigs had previously hung there. All the villagers proper had a pig spike in their outhouse; but on the hills about six miles away the custom differed. The cottagers there used a strong pole instead; the end of the pole fitted the pig's jaw; the carcase was hung on the pole and thus held aslant against a wall. The legs on either side of the pole gave the whole thing a look of a pig climbing a pole.

The cutting up of the carcase was done the following morning, when the butcher arrived with cleaver, knife, saw, and steel-yard scales. First the carcase was to be weighed whole; but what it was going to weigh was always a matter of conjecture beforehand. To judge the weight of a pig wisely required much knowledge, a sense of its size and substance gained only through long experience. Many villagers prided themselves on their ability, others were modest and doubtful, but none would pass without stopping to make some forecast, which, I noticed, was usually a score pounds less than the actual weight. Father never contradicted them, as many would have done. He understood the country mind and knew what a delicate matter it was to question the findings of wisdom, especially on such a subject as the probable weight of a pig.

At that time no house would have seemed complete without its pig form. They were made by the local carpenter, of thick elm plank into which strong oak legs were tenoned. A V-shaped channel was carved along the middle of the top, joined by oblique channels on each side. The form served to kill the pig on, afterwards for the cutting up, then to lay the flitches on for salting. The salting was done in the darkness of a cellar, where the form remained till the next pig wanted it.

The butcher, lifting the carcase from the scales, laid it on the form, and straightway cut off the head. This he divided into halves; then severed the ears and extracted the eyes. I was bidden to fetch a saucer, in which I carried the brains to my mother, who was already busily preparing for the joints that would soon be taken indoors. Then the carcase was cut into halves; it was our custom to have the backbone taken out separately. After that, the hams, gammons, spare ribs, haseletts, griskins, and rearings, all were cut, leaving the two flitches robbed of bones, in shape and condition for salting. A curious item was the extraction of a muscle from each flitch, called "the mouse".

He who has not tasted backbone pie has missed a minor delight. Who can describe the delicious compound of jelly and sweet flesh that lay beneath that homely roof of crust? We always ate them cold, and folk to-day, who long ago dined with us by chance at such times, still declare that never before nor since have they known such enjoyment. Yet the delicacy of backbone pie was challenged by the famous turnover pies, made by my mother from the oddments of flesh and trimmings from the joints. No one else knew, nor could she explain when asked, as she often was, "how she made them so nice?" She had no secret recipe, no special knowledge of spices; it was "a little bit of this, that and the other" — the kidneys and the melt and a cutting from the liver, all savoury food, chopped up together with sweet fresh pork, solidly packed and heaped within the rolled-out circle of dough, which she folded over and plaited along the top from end to end. When they were made, they were ranged side by side and end to end, in one long shallow tin tray, and so passed into the large brick oven. There they slowly cooked, sizzling in their own gravy, which permeated the bottom crust and left it richly plastic. These also we ate cold. Sometimes it was at Christmas time, when relatives and friends were there to share them. Our youthful appetites had been sharpened again by a spell on the ice, for it seems we always had ice at Christmas in those far-off days. The pressure of the knife on those pies revealed no cavity, no pretentious space. It was a clean cut, solid from top to bottom, the piece cut off like a fragment of tessellated paving, a mosaic of glutinous meats enclosed within a square of honest crust. If we tired of them — as one does even of the best of food — there were faggots to fall back on for a change. They were compounds of chopped liver and kidneys, made up into balls within a wrapping of thin skin, called the *caul*. They also were cooked in a large tray in the brick oven; thick veins of fat interlaced the caul, travelling over and round the faggots in fascinating patterns.

It was difficult to pass pig-killing without a bilious attack; but such minor troubles were only part of the occasion and were quickly forgotten.

The main purpose of the pig was apparent in the two large flitches that eventually adorned the cottage walls — "the purtiest picture in the house" — as we used to say. To understand why, you must know not only the labourer's habit of mind but the poverty from which his stock had sprung. Yet who could dread the privations of winter with such provision at hand ? What solidity of fat, what streaks of lean were there! It was good to put the knife into it and feel its firm resistance; to cut off the food for the day and to prove by trial its sustenance for work, howsoever hard; its staying influence, no matter how bad the weather. The real "home-cured" had its established place in the lives of every villager of old time; whether on the home table or under the thumb in the bleak open field; whether boiled in cubes, or fried in rashers, or cut into shreds and rolled between dough, made ragged with suet and eaten cold in the form of a long solid dumpling. The old villagers retained this faith in bacon until death, but the young inclined to beef and mutton. It thus followed that, in due time, it ceased to be the staple food of the village.

The marvellous quality of that bacon is now only a memory. How we loved it! I have been told that the secret lay in the home feeding of the pig, the variety of its food and the wholesome barley meal with which it was fatted. Certain it is that no bacon to-day seems to equal it.

CHAPTER
SEVEN

Duck Breeding

The village has never been quite the same since the cottagers stopped breeding ducks for the London market. Once they were so much a part of our life that we could not have imagined the ponds and greens without them. The ponds now look forsaken, as though themselves admitting that they have ceased to serve their true purpose. Their waters once so clear are turbid and overgrown with weeds, and the beautiful pool in front of the church goes dry in the summer, as if in despair, as it rarely did when ducks sported there.

Except when snow covered the ground, and the water froze, so that they could not wash themselves, our ducks' large pure white bodies were a pleasant sight. Whether on the ponds, tail up and head down, seeking some morsel in the mud at the bottom; or with flapping wings, chasing each other across the surface in a gambol of ecstasy; or sailing about in mass formation, each with neck erect and head forwards; their movements were always graceful. Or, when in some wayside ditch they foraged, or on an April morning caught the large worms that lay half-way out of the earth on the village greens, their lives seemed to be ever infused with the proper village spirit — a rollicky, happy-go-lucky, carefree sort of existence, free from any concern for the morrow and happy in the provision of the moment.

Their gait on land was perfectly matched to the even tenor of the village life. Each morning they walked its ways in line — the father drake, with his six to eight wives. He always led the way; they followed on behind; his eyes were always casting to right and left to know if the way was free from danger. It was delightful to watch that waddling line of white passing over the carpet of deep green, every neck and body zigzagging with every step. The sway sideways was caused by the weight of the bodies, which were large and had deep keels between short legs. One look showed how out of poise the body must be when momentarily supported by one leg or the other in the act of walking. It could only be done at all by alternately throwing the whole weight over from side to side. The drake and his retinue of ducks were selections from the batch of the previous year, and were called a *clutch*. They were chosen and retained for breeding; or, to be more exact, they produced the eggs, which were always hatched by hens. In the laying season every duck faithfully laid one egg every day. The owner kept them all imprisoned until this duty had been done. There, loudly quacking, with only a rude door between themselves and freedom, they impatiently demanded his arrival. He waited only to see the last egg laid; then he opened the door, and a mad scramble began, which quickly settled down into the proper, regular march in line, as, led by the drake, all headed together for their distant pond.

That was the daily march, so much a part of the life to which we all grew up that no one imagined it would ever cease to be. The ponds were the common meeting-places; clutches of various owners met there and swam as one community for the day. The passion and glory of their life being swimmable water, they made what haste ducks could, always pausing at a chance puddle on the way to dip each bill once as they went by. But should danger of dog or other fearsome form be seen, then the march in line changed to a medley of disorder till the worst was passed, when each tail would wag at once in confident assurance; and the march would be resumed. As soon as the pond came into view, their gait quickened; the waddle became a run for the margin, where all lined up and drank to the day ahead, each filling its broad bill and raising its head to feel water's cool flow down the throat.

They assembled clutch by clutch, the first-comers ever ready to welcome those that followed. The drakes knew no jealousy. When they saw another clutch approaching, they swam to the margin to welcome them. The pond was their citadel of safety, a domain of their own, free from the intrusion of man or beast. On sunny days and dreary days alike, their quacking s still sounded like a note of joy. There, while the hours stole by, and children's voices from the school made melody in hymn and song, everybody's ducks swam together, or gambolled to and fro, or dived, or lay at ease on the broad-spreading grass.

So the day passed — its hours told off by the old bell within the grey church tower; and martins wheeled round in flight all day or, swerving, skimmed the water's surface for the fly, or sought its brink for mud for building nests. Those hours seemed much the same except for the changing numbers counted out by the deep toned-bell. Yet the ducks knew their time, whether by bell or some inward sense, and at their hour they left the pond and formed again in clutch.

Then eastward, westward, northward, long swaying lines of white were seen, each line a drake with his ducks behind him treading through the deep-grown grass. All their diverging pathways led from pond to home, a rough shed with corn and straw within for food and rest.

At the cottage homesteads to which they all were going, a very different order of duck life was going forward. There ducklings of all ages up to eight or ten weeks were to be seen, penned in shallow enclosures on the garden ground. The pens were made of thin boards about eighteen inches high, fixed edgewise by stakes. The cottagers came to our yard to buy them. When making the pens, you had to be very careful not to leave any crevice through which a duckling could pass its head and commit accidental suicide. They lived a precarious, delicate life that demanded incessant watchfulness. Intense sunshine on their heads would turn them giddy; so there had to be some protective awning or board under which they could creep. An unexpected shower that wetted their feathers was dangerous in another way: for warmth afterwards they were inclined to huddle together and thus contract chills; so they were kept on the move after a shower until the feathers had dried.

A stock duck seldom showed any desire to hatch her own eggs. Indeed, it seemed to be in keeping with their care-free dispositions that hens should do it for them. Sitting hens, for sale or hire, were in great demand throughout the season; heavy crossbreeds, with some feather on the legs, were preferred. The orange box, with its three compartments, was largely used for setting, one hen on thirteen duck eggs to each part. The boxes were placed end to end in rows on the floor of a shed specially assigned for that purpose. Silence reigned; scores of hens in semi-darkness sat out their four weeks of parental durance.

The task was really nothing but an imposition; for after faithfully sitting and hatching the young ducks, the hen was rarely allowed to have them for more than a day or so. She was turned adrift in the run instead, and the ducklings were kept in a shallow box and fed with hard-boiled egg chopped up with boiled rice, to which a little fine meal was added. It was imperative that a saucer of water should be at hand for them to wet their bills in. Throughout the eight or ten weeks of their lives feeding was graded according to their advance in size. When they were large enough, scalded greaves, the residue of the tallow-chandler — mixed with pollard and, later on, barley meal — became the staple food with which they gorged themselves and rapidly put on delicate flesh. Enclosed in the pens they had little exercise, and their proneness to eating soon made them lazy with weight. The body became too large for the strength of the legs. Filled with good food, they drowsed away the greater part of the few weeks that constituted their lives; to them an experience of ease, sunshine, and plenty.

When they were about half-grown, they were driven to a pond to have their one and only swim, which helped them to feather properly. It was not unusual to meet a flock that covered the whole road from side to side, each a little ball of yellow fluff, merrily chirping as it walked. There were no motor cars in those days, and the horse-drawn vehicle simply had to stop until they had passed. Unlike chickens, they were easily controlled; their disposition was to keep together in a flock, and they always appeared to be enjoying themselves. The owners had their special call, "Dill! Dill! Dill!" for ducklings, in imitation of the sounds that they made. The call was not used when they grew older.

It was a treat to see them all take the water; to watch them head off bravely over its surface, then dive and flap their little wings in natural delight. That was one of the few pleasures of duck breeding, but those who had the responsibility in hand declared that all the rest was incessant work and worry. "Ducking" — as the industry was called — was "nothing but moil and groil, work from light to dark, for as long as the season lasted."

And this was true: it was no light matter to be responsible for some hundreds of young lives; to attend to their parents — the sitting hens — daily; to take over the charge of the newly hatched young; to cook their food as they grew older; to clean and prepare the pens and guard against emergencies, housing them safely each night on clean straw. At the same time, there were the fully grown to be killed and plucked ready for market. This was done in the early morning, and after plucking they were placed in a cold chamber to cool off before being packed for transit by rail. Many labourers' wives, I knew, did all this alone, except for occasional help of women at the plucking, for which they were paid three-halfpence a duck. Their husbands were away at regular work on a farm, and could only lend a hand in the evening. The money that ducking brought in was hardly earned, for often the price dropped as low as half a crown per head. Yet some folk saved enough by it to buy their own cottages; and now and then the thriftiest made it their first stepping stone to rise above the position of a labourer, and eventually to take land on their own as small farmers.

The ducks for market were collected late each afternoon. A large cob, drawing a covered cart, which had a trundling sound that we all recognized as the duckman, went round the district, delivering empty hampers called *flats*, and collecting others filled with dead ducks. The duckman acted as agent for the Smithfield salesmen and issued their consignment notes to the breeders, one of which stating the number of ducks and name of the owner, was placed in each hamper. He paid over the money on a subsequent call, handing to each breeder a salesman's voucher of the price made, from which his own agent's fee was deducted. The demand was at its best when green peas were in season; and so the aim of each breeder was to catch the early market.

A cottage garden given over to duck breeding was not an inviting sight, and the stench after a warm June shower was even worse to put up with. Hard work, worry, and bad smell; no wonder the village held ducking mildly in disrepute; so that the dwellers in what was properly called *Duck Lane* changed the name to *Flint Street* instead. A local sickness called "duck fever" was formerly prevalent; it was said to come from the smell of the ducklings. No matter what efforts were made to keep them clean, the paddling feet of the young ducks, and their continual need of water, caused the pens to be always dirty with slime. And one villager would say to another over duck-pens: "I wonder what those who'll eat them would say if they could see the places where they are bred."

CHAPTER EIGHT

Allotments

It would be unbelievable, if it were not true, that in the redistribution of the land at the enclosure of 1830, no provision was made for allotments to be let to the poor. When all that can be has been said in defence of that revolution in ancient village life, the simple bare fact stands out, a revelation of the callous disregard of the landless labourer, and evidence of his utterly degraded condition.

It would have been simple for Parliament, when passing the separate Acts of Enclosure, to insert a condition that lands made over to the Church in lieu of tithes should be available for allotments for the poor at a just rental, if required. But such matters were left to the discretion of those in authority in each parish. The consequence in my village was that, for some forty years after, the cottagers could not get even a plot on which to grow their own vegetables.

No special knowledge of the villagers is necessary to understand what a loss this must have been. But they patiently submitted; Botany Bay and Van Diemen's Land (if not the gallows) were then only too familiarly associated with rebellion. It is well to remember that the daily work of these men was cultivating the land of others, on a large parish of over three thousand acres, yet never before or since was so much food produced from the soil, and the producers so hungry.

Just about the time of my birth, however, one or two small fields were first subdivided into roods to be let, and these were all eagerly taken by the poor. Their characters were not demoralized by it; indeed their lives were more orderly and law-abiding. The notion that a plot of land would make them inconveniently independent was shaken; it was more than counterbalanced by the relief it afforded to a poverty that was painful to witness.

Corn growing was not paying so well as it had done, and so the demand for land became easier. Eighteen acres of glebe land, that had been let at two pounds an acre, was offered by the Vicar to the labourers at one pound per rood (later on reduced to fifteen shillings) and they rejoiced at getting it so cheap. Other owners followed suit; one man, who posed as a leader of village morality, let off a small field at ninepence a pole. The labourers did resent this charge, and their resentment came to a head when he refused to provide a new gate to the field. A political meeting, at which he sat on the platform, gave them a chance to express their feelings. Politics and matters of national importance were drowned by shouts of "Ninepence a pole!" "Ninepence a pole! and find your own gate!" The allotments had become a most important part of the cottager's life. A stock of potatoes could now be grown and stored against each winter; it became possible to grow and fat a pig and to hang its flitches on

the cottage walls. To these ends every available hour —
except Sunday — throughout the spring, summer, and
autumn was given to their cultivation; and often, when
the work was in arrears, the husband would rise early
and put in an hour or two before beginning labour on the
farm at seven.

The allotment fields of the village resembled the
preceding open-field system; the rood strips, side by
side, were, in miniature, like the former acre strips.
Throughout the long summer evenings, someone would
be seen working on each, often husband and wife with
the older children of the family. Many roods were
planted with corn — wheat for the family loaves and
puddings, or barley for the pig in the sty; but the potato
crop was important beyond any other. Many labourers
rented two or more roods, and thus were able to grow
both corn and vegetables. In that way the standard of life
was improved; but it is clear at the same time that it
made it possible to accept the less-than-living-wage for
longer than it would otherwise have lasted.

The plots were cultivated well, and the rents were
properly paid. It was, in fact, an order of life that proved
natural to them all. The sacrifice and toil involved
brought a new outlook on life; to become the tenant of
the rood of land, though by payment of rent, was an act
of independence that found a ready response in native
character; it preserved a meaning to life above that of
merely working for a wage.

The spirit of co-operation developed. As their
forefathers, on the open-field system, had joined hands
to withstand excessive manorial demands, so the

allotment holders made joint appeal for reductions of rents. It was not possible for that side-by-side cultivation to continue without convincing each holder that the interest of one was the interest of all.

Later on, a sympathetic government directed the County Council to foster the spirit of co-operation by lectures, and to aid co-operative purchase of seeds and fertilizers. So the small-holdings movement came into operation. Some allotment holders were in a position to avail themselves of its advantages, and many hoped and expected that in due course something like the pre-enclosure peasantry would again be established on the soil.

Only through co-operation could those small plot holders hope to conform to the methods of agriculture then being practised. To dig the rood of land and to broadcast it with seed, wheat or barley, and to cut the crop by hand labour when ripe, involved little more than their personal labour. To thresh it, however, was a different matter, so they co-operated in the hire of threshing engine and machine, for which small stacks of corn from separate allotments were stacked in order on a plot near the gateway. Threshing day was a lively sight and so was the day following, when each owner was tying his straw into trusses and carting it away for bedding the pig in the sty.

A feeling grew up that the co-operative spirit needed a convivial expression. The harvest-home suppers at the farms had long ago been dropped; the allotment holders decided to have one on their own. The village had always had its local leaders, men with a natural turn for leadership, who, having themselves known the pinch of penury early in life, ceased not to advocate the cause of the labourer. They were not slow to act and to take on responsibility. A committee was formed and subscriptions from sympathizers came in. The wives entered into the scheme with spirit; they cooked huge plum puddings, and vegetables, and joints of beef roast. Each holder contributed to the common feast either a small sum of money or some produce from his land. The spread was laid forth in a large barn; and on a late autumn evening they all assembled; there they fell to with appetites and thirsts that quantity could never daunt. Speeches were made by the leaders, about the land and all that it meant to rural life. George, to whom the event was a floodlit joy, sang once again his time-honoured song, *Life's a Bumper*.

This was the village spirit. It remained unaffected by the making of a main-line railway near the village, but strangely enough it disappeared with the great war. Why this happened is beyond the power of this pen to write. The clearest evidence that the old village spirit is no more lies in the fact that it is now difficult to find tenants for the allotments. Yet one may incline to believe that if only the movement for reinstating the small peasantry on the land had come about a generation earlier than it did, the war would have found them attached to their holdings and wedded to the soil.

CHAPTER
NINE

Going Uppards

At the time of my youth the flat stretches of Middlesex intervening between the village and distant London were all grass lands, dotted with isolated farmsteads, or here and there a small village. Where, recently with almost mushroom growth, large up-to-date factories and modern townships have sprung up, was then a large area of undeveloped country, which produced the hay for the multitude of horses that travelled the London streets, and for the dairy cows that supplied milk to its people.

Every day, within a radius of some thirty miles from the city, large carts and wagons piled with hay wended their way there, and returned on the following day loaded with manure that could be obtained in London in plenty, almost for the asking. This cheap and plentiful source of replenishment for the Middlesex soil made it possible for a crop to be taken away each season. The district was called the hay country. Cartage by road held on long after railways were established, and hay and straw continued to be sent, and even from greater distances.

For the greater part of the year those flat expanses of land were quiet and lonely. Cattle grazed the fields after

118

the crop had been taken off; the ricks were cut up and sent away; the hedges were trimmed and mended and the dykes cleaned out. But all such work involved little total labour and the comparatively few men permanently employed in the hay country were quite unable to cope with the sudden large amount of work that had to be done quickly when the year's crop of grass was ready to cut.

Each hay season, therefore, wandering labourers flocked there from London and the country around. Men of our village went regularly and always found employment at once; for the men of Bucks were known, and preferred to those from the town. They started out early on a Monday morning, men in groups of three or four who had agreed together to take mowing by the piece, in co-operation. They knew one another's capabilities, each would be able to maintain the pace, and at the same time to cut a swathe of the normal width; each, in short, would fairly deserve his earnings. They called this migration *going uppards*. If anyone asked for them after they had left the village the reply would be "Gone uppards", for everyone was sure to know what that meant.

They carried their scythes with them; blades of proven steel, ground ready, wrapped in old sacking, and carried separate from the curved *sneds* with their handles attached. The ring attachments and wedges, and a hammer to tighten them with, were taken along in a basket, where also they stored the whetstone, or *rubber*. Each knew that in the long and strenuous task ahead the scythe was the essential co-operator; they knew its "right

119

hang" to a nicety, the angle at which it would cut the heaviest swathe with the least effort. And yet, when they had arranged all to the last degree of perfection, they knew themselves in for a long spell of hard work, for many days of long sustained effort in which the bodily frame would learn to be an automaton, unconscious of fatigue.

The separation, too, from home and village was real enough. Practical mementoes of home life — food to last the first few days, and a change of underwear — were taken to the cart that was hired to take them all the way. Everybody knew that none of them would come back before the work was finished, and the chance of news of them and their welfare was very uncertain. Even if they could write they were not likely to be inclined to; their time was to be filled with work, drink, food, and rest: and so the wives had to assume that they were all right and that they would return with their earnings when the time came.

They slept on shakedowns of straw or hay in the out-buildings of the farmsteads. Beer was supplied free and in plenty — large barrels of mild, which were renewed as fast as emptied. Thus the sweat the scythemen lost on the fields was renewed from large earthenware bottles of beer, which they carried with them to work each morning. The quantity drunk was enormous; old Johnnie would boast of the time when he disposed of sixteen horns at the first sitting down. They went to their shakedown every night as full of beer as they could go, and thought nothing of it. Beer was some consolation for the separation from wife, family, and native village.

Every Sunday they cooked food in the open, and at odd times they washed and dried a shirt.

In the field they worked in formation, the best mower leading and setting the pace, the others following at proper distances apart. The action was alike in all, a strong, broad sweep from right to left with a short step forward; a rhythmical action of perfect beauty that appeared to require no effort, so perfectly was it done. Each man left his mown lane cut clean from side to side, his swathe of cut grass in billowy line, just as their fathers had mown in centuries past.

They knew the advantage of the dewy morning and evening; the hours of sunrise and decline, when the moistened grass was *rim* to the cut. Then the air was cool, and fragrant with the exhalations of growth at its summer zenith; it was the time to get the work forward, to cut the most grass with the least effort. The mid-day heat dried the halm and made it harsh to the scythe; that was the time for a good long rest and sleep.

Their advance never ceased, except during those hours of rest. They changed the landscape as they moved; the far-spread waving grass became billowy lines of fragrant hay. The air grew sweet with its scent; but it was an all-pervading sweetness from which there was no escape; pleasant at first, it became in time satiating.

Others went from the village besides those who went as mowers; many helped at the making and the carrying of the hay. They were paid by the day. They followed the mowers from field to field, tedding and turning the swathes, and finally carting the dried hay to the stacks. These haymakers worked through the heat of the day, so as to get the hay in when it was warm with the sun. The half-built stacks, often with large sheets hung over them on a pole, offered inviting beds for the night to the casual labourer that came by. Yet to sleep on one was fraught with danger. Old George told the tales of a dead man discovered in a rick when it was cut for market; and of a careful farm mistress, who sent every night to make sure that no one was sleeping on them before she went to bed for the night herself.

Home going was a joyous day to the exiled workers, and even more so (because of the unexpectedness) to the family in the village. The wife, the children, the cottage, with its garden, had never once been absent from the father's thoughts. Once, I was told, they arrived home in the dead of night. They had travelled by rail, and walked from a distant station, and when they got home all were abed and asleep. Now it so happened that the family of one of the returning mowers had lived out his long absence on short commons, having had hardly enough to eat the whole time. The news that father was back with money in his pocket woke them all up at once; they all got up and dressed, some to kindle the fire, others to knock up the butcher and the baker from their sleep. Fry and bread was bought and cooked then and there, and deep in the night the reunited family sat down at last to a glorious feed.

CHAPTER
TEN

The Market

Going to market always brought with it a spirit of hilarity as well it might, for a good deal of real drudgery belonged to village life. To put on clean clothes and lighter boots was itself an aid and inspiration to the spirit. Besides, however much one loved the village and enjoyed its life, to get away from it once a week; for a few hours made it seem all the pleasanter on the return. And so the weekly market, though it was fundamentally a business matter, had a character beyond mere buying and selling; it was also a good-humoured gathering and meeting together, everybody expected this and responded to it heartily.

The drive there was generally cheerful and lively, for as often as not the wife would decide to join the husband and take a child or two along, until the thing became indeed a family party. They joined the erratic procession on the road, all going to market: the carrier's four-wheel van drawn by a trotting cob, the whole space under its tilt-roof packed with wide-eyed faces, all looking forward; up-to-date, thriving farmers in knee breeches and gaiters, seated wide-legged in smart gigs and driving spanking horses; farm carts, which had known their last coat of paint long ago, covered over with pig nets made of strong cord, with pigs underneath the net, or maybe a few fat sheep for sale — all these, together with younger men on bicycles, and a few walking.

The market town welcomed them all with outspread arms, and properly so, for it seemed to do more trade on that one day of the week than on all the other days put together. Already the joints at *The King of the Air* were sizzling in their own gravy, likewise at *The Queen of the Water* and the *Horses* both *Black* and *White*. Each of these houses (and others not mentioned) had its special fraternity of farmers and smallholders, men of like disposition and financial status, who dined where they had always dined and would not think of going elsewhere, for they found good fellowship and good cheer there, and enjoyed it with a freedom equal to home. At market neighbours who had lived all their lives only a few doors apart in the same village, found it convenient at last to settle up business matters; in fact, the meeting at market was the recognized place for all taking and paying of money and endorsing of accounts. The whole atmosphere, wholly different from that of the open field and the farm, conspired to that end.

Outside in the market-place a motley crowd jostled; squires and farmers of almost equal status strode amongst yokels who had driven in cattle and sheep and pigs from the farms and were waiting to know what they would have to drive back. Massed together they made a joyous mixture, with country good humour in evidence everywhere.

"An how be *you* getting on?" would be heard a hundred times, and so would the reply, "Well, I has enough to eat and drink and I sleeps warm a-nights, so I suppose I've got no cause to grumble."

Smaller clusters of the crowd stood listening and laughing, round the London cheapjack whose bold, free speaking and superior self-assurance stood him out in vivid contrast in such country company. I remember how a man who sold cough mixture described the chemist's shop, and sarcastically dwelt upon the long names in Latin painted up on the row of drawers beyond the counter. "Burnt sugar!" he cried scornfully; "burnt sugar, and powdered chalk!" "All done", said he, "to mystify you. But I'll tell you one thing they always take care to put in plain English — *the bill you have to pay!*" And so he got his laugh and sold his own mysterious mixture.

Lively and hard-working, these cheapjacks and salesmen seemed to be there to provide the chief amusement at market, yet they did enough trade meanwhile, or why did they come again and again? The shop-keepers, too, were out for their share of the spoils, with goods displayed outside their own shops on extempore stalls over the gutter; and corn merchants came in for trade from other towns, ranging their trays of samples out before *The King of the Air*.

Yet all these were only side-lines; the real business of the day, the backbone of the gathering, was to be seen among the massed pens of pigs, sheep, and calves that partially blocked the broad open street, and among the herds of cattle waiting for the auctioneer's ring. Each section here seemed to have its own fraternity; the crowd about the pigs seemed different from the crowd about

125

the cattle. Each auctioneer had his own personality too, as well known to the buyers as was his clear ringing voice, heard above the babel of men and cattle. And the auctioneer knew his buyers, and the type of cattle or sheep, fat or lean stores, that each would bid for. His eye was quick to catch at times the sly wink from a face held purposely behind the head of another buyer. It was his personality, if any, that seemed to rule the market.

All was an ordered confusion, each noisy group was really fulfilling its part in the life of the whole; the squealing of pigs, as they were unloaded and reloaded into carts, was a proper part of the market, and so was the lowing of calves. Now and then there was a sudden rush, as the crowd ran helter-skelter before cattle in a panic, to whom the whole ordeal of market must have been a terrifying experience. All together formed a single sound — the song of the market — voices of men and beasts from far-away farms, from hills and from valleys, all mixing and mingling, all rising and falling together — the pride of the town.

It did not last long: just a few hours of that medley of man and beast, of chatter, laughter, and a kind of care-free attitude into which entered keen bargain hunting and astute dealings, and much drinking of healths. Market achieved the social interlinking of the people of a far spread district of isolated farms, hamlets, and villages; it was the one focus to which all interests in common converged; a natural concourse, of hoary antiquity and still supplying an absolute need. All who met at market, though they did not know it perhaps, were there by ancient tradition; in their ride to the town and home again they followed the march of their fathers and were still a part of the stream that had flowed on for ages between village and town.

There, for a while, the ties of home are forgotten — the claims of the farm, the land, and the dairy. Yet this not for long. For the nag at the stable strains hard at the halter; the ostler is waiting (his claim is but sixpence, and a tip if good nature prevails); then "hie-oh" for home, the farm, and the village; their needs reassume their proportions. The mind is uneasy; the thought is of duties that wait to be done: of the cattle, the poultry, the pigs and the sheep, all waiting attention, all bleating, all calling — the cries that for ages have found a response in the heart of the yeoman — all there in the meadows, the hovels, the stables; all there to be fed, to be littered and watered, ere the mind can be easy.

So off for the farm and the village! The nag needs no urging; "Good-day" from the ostler; the rattle of wheels on the fair cobble road. A pair of clean heels and the miles are as nothing; so join the procession, all going, all leaving, some slower, some faster, all going one way. The town is forsaken; it clears up the rubbish, it brightens its pathways, it counts up its money, and broods, half asleep, till the next market day.

CHAPTER
ELEVEN

Rag, Tag, and Bobtail

The village always had its funny folk — natives and descendants of natives for centuries, to whom the village was all sufficient, and life anywhere else unthinkable.

It may be that they represented the original village stock far better than the more orthodox majority, whose habits led to no unconventional reputation; or perhaps they were the interesting results of a limited marriage circle, by which their definite qualities of character and disposition had been emphasized and perpetuated.

They were invariably poor; it seemed natural to us that they should be so, and they themselves showed no hope nor wish to be anything else. Sometimes they were near to destitution, yet their lives looked happy and they never lost their humour; they had the knack of seeing the funny side of misfortunes, a droll speech and ways that were always amusing to the rest of us.

As birds of a feather, they dwelt together in one small colony in a group of cottages hidden away behind larger homes; the common entrance to the colony was through a narrow gangway, walled and roofed and known as "up the tunnel". There was nothing noticeable about the entrance to the tunnel, and newcomers often lived for a long time in the village without knowing of the cottages to which it led.

There lived John with his wife Mercia and their children, who all inherited their father's unique outlook on life, as well as his witticism and happy nature. There, in bachelor seclusion, also lived the renowned Harry Stranks, a tailor and a philosopher, whose reply to all questions other wise unanswerable was "That's the point". He undertook to reveal all mysteries and left it to his hearers to test his ability with questions. "How then, is it", they asked him, "that the cleverest men are often the biggest fools?" Harry meditated his reply. "Ah, that's the point", he said.

John and Harry were neighbours whose cottages were attached, a detail which bothered neither of them. Late one Saturday evening (it was late autumn and the village was all a-buzz with harvest earnings) George, a blustering native of mischievous disposition,, had felt the need of harvest fun. Well primed with cheer, he had called on Harry to suggest that they should spend the evening together. Harry was against the idea; he pointed out that his cottage was a poor place, not to be recommended for social enjoyment. George made light of such apologies; outsides alone, he said, were all he cared for. And he imposed himself at Harry's hearth; he made the room cheery at once by heaping on the fire a pile of bean stubble that poor Harry had carefully collected. But the chimney, foul with long use and lack of cleaning, and quite unaccustomed to such a blaze, very quickly caught fire. It flamed like a volcano, lighting up all that part of the village, and neighbours

129

came flocking up the tunnel, expecting to find the cottages themselves consumed George cleared off, well satisfied with his exploit.

Through the bedroom window of the adjoining cottage Mercia might be seen shaking her spouse, John, who had had a harvest meal himself and had gone to bed early, and was now enjoying his first sleep. Her voice came out to the watchers: "Wake up! Wake up! and get out of the house before ye be burned alive." She had not been gifted with her husband's disposition; and had no patience with his unalarmed demeanour and his drowsy reply, "Surely, Mercy; 'tis not so urgent as all that!" She was for immediate action; she insisted on it. At last the dangerous truth had stirred him; but there remained the problem of getting him dressed. He called for his clothes item after item, as Mercia, to the amusement of all the village outside, found them and helped him to put them on. Presently there was a serious hitch; his trusty belt could not be found, it had fallen into some dark part of the bedroom. Mercia urged that this was no time to trouble about belts; "Far better lose it", said she, "than have all the furniture burned." But John was adamant; he couldn't at that moment bear the thought of life without the belt that had served him so many years. "Find me my belt," shouted he; "then out goes the nolls."

By the time the belt was found the blaze had died down and danger was past.

John always looked at life calmly like this; but Mercia was given to anxiety. Once, in the dead of night, she roused him, swearing that robbers were in the house. "I told her to lie quiet", he said. "I told her, so soon as they touched anything *very* valuable, I'd spring out and surprise them!" This was how he put it to his fellow-workers the following day, and they quoted it to his credit for quite fifty years after. They knew the inside of his cottage; they saw the joke.

Once, when he could find no work in the village, he made up his mind to seek it elsewhere. Mercia helped to get him ready for the quest, but strongly objected to the flail that he proposed taking with him.

"So sure as you take that", said she, "there will be trouble."

"Nay, Mercy", replied John, "who knows but what it will be just the very thing to get me a job? I may likely find an old-fashioned farmer who wants a bit of corn tapped out."

When well away, he called at a shop to buy something to eat. The people in the shop had never seen a flail before. John explained that it was a flail, for threshing corn. They wanted to know exactly how a flail was used. John, ever obliging, swung it round in correct style, when, alas! its far end hit some jugs that were hung from the ceiling, and brought them crashing to the floor. John was man enough afterwards to admit that Mercia's prophecy came true.

Scores of similar stories formerly circulated about the village, though many are now forgotten. They were re-told many times, but their power to amuse seemed to be unfailing. Everyone told the tale of Bold Harry White, who one wintry morning, seeing the snow knee deep outside his window, turned to his wife, still snugly in bed, and cried out: "What a morning this is to have to go out to work in, Sally!" "Not half so bad", she replied, "as stopping at home and wondering how to pay the rent!"

He put their difference impartially before his fellow-labourers as they all plodded to work. They remembered it to his renown. He was a short man, venerable to look at, with his long beard and grave demeanour and general air of one whose mind was conversant with the wisdom of sages. He had a keen sense of humour and delighted to make others laugh, yet rarely smiled himself. Why he was called Bold Harry I never learned, and now no one seems to know.

Such stories of such persons enlivened the drabness of toil and gave colour to old village life. There humour was as natural as a spring, it bubbled up and found expression close at hand, in the sayings and doings of this and that one, neighbours whose life histories were known and whose peculiarities of disposition were understood. Every telling of a stock anecdote, besides bringing a laugh, called up a mental picture of the man himself — often dead long ago — the original whimsical manner, and form and style of speech, all contributing to the enjoyment.

It would be folly to say how many times George* actually told me the story of Sam and the toad, gaily each time and as though it was the very first time of telling.

When he was a boy, George said, he went with a farmer shooting over his farm. By and by, George said,

* For George, see Chapter XII.

they came to a hedge, and Sam was known to be cleaning out the ditch on the other side. Hearing his voice in conversation, the farmer motioned silence, stole quietly up to the old man, and asked who he was talking to? Sam was taken by surprise, "Oh, master," said he, "I didn't know as you was anywhere a-nigh, I was only a-talking to an old toad, asking him how he fared; I see him here, ten years ago, when last I cleaned out the ditch."

Sam's job just then was solitary in the extreme; men would often work at such tasks as his all day without any human association. The mind ruminated on the things that could be seen, the birds and animals of the fields, the advance or decline of the signs of the season, or the changing weather. They knew the time to within a few minutes by the position of the sun, or the strength of light or the condition of the atmosphere, or even, when nesting was over, by the return of the rooks to their colony.

Time had a different quality to such people, and memory was their chief calendar. Seeing a labourer laying a hedge, I remarked that it was a long time since it was last laid.

"Forty years", answered he straightway.

"Someone remembers, then", said I.

"Yes, Ben remembers."

Or speaking to a farmer who had just retired, I expressed a sentimental regret for the wagons ranged side by side at his sale, each with the family name on its front board. I said that it seemed like turning old servants adrift to see them go. I knew that he would know their histories, and I was not surprised to be told of one that it had been purchased second-hand, seventy years before; that an old man of his village had helped when a boy to draw it to the farm, where it had remained ever since.

How very much the old English farm was a life separate to itself with a yearly routine that varied little! Dependence on the weather ensured that exceptional seasons — seasons cold, wet, or dry — were all remembered; for all were part of the farmer's very life, His was the mind that understood the character and qualities of the soil here and there on the farm; it was no more than natural to him to know the ancestry of his horses and livestock. Every implement had its history; when it was bought, for instance, and who made it.

There were a few men in the village who could not be classed as day labourers; they seemed to have the pre-enclosure spirit in their dispositions, and would never settle to work for a weekly wage. They loved a small plot of land on their own; they would keep a few pigs, a clutch of ducks, some fowls, and perhaps a calf, at their cottage homesteads, which resembled miniature farms. Often they kept a donkey, or an old pony, with cart and harness bought second-hand at market or some local sale.

Everything about them and their premises showed a careful avoidance of expenditure. The sheds were usually built by themselves of wichert and stone walls, with over-layer roof on horizontal timbers, heaped to the ridge with brushwood, hedge-trimmings and halm, and covered with thatch. The last coat of paint had long ago peeled and powdered off the cart; the harness was never a complete set. Small owners of this type were never sensitive about appearance; it often suited purpose better to look like a poor but industrious man, out to make a living in any way that offered.

How the living was made was understood only by the man who made it; to everybody else it was more or less of a mystery. Some of us looked upon them as men willing to do a job at an agreed price when needed, and willing to take useless junk away in part payment. To others they were sellers of faggots, or buyers of eggs and sitting hens when duck breeding was in season. They always seemed to have a plump chicken for sale if one or other of the villagers wanted one suddenly. They grew vegetables and corn on their allotments, and they lived on this, and the salted pig, and sold what they themselves did not need. Each year they sent a few score ducks to London; they also kept a breeding sow which farrowed twice a year, the sale of its young being an important part of their fortune.

They could turn their hands to almost all the work of a farm, and were ready to help at a push in the hay or harvest field. The farmers liked this; it suited the purpose of both to be on good terms; and the farmer would lend a heavy horse and cart, or plough an allotment, in exchange for manual help when needed.

Now and then one of those who led this semi-independent life would do better for himself than the rest and become a farmer. By continually using his own wits, by never-ceasing thrift, a few pounds were bound to be saved. This money was held waiting till an opportunity came of renting a few acres, and when the acres were secured all the family devoted their whole time, thought, and effort to the land. They knew it was to be sink or swim with them, and were certain of a long wait before a return could be expected, so every penny that could be spared was saved to help tide over the months of labour and expenditure that preceded harvest.

To others the fascination of "dealing" surpassed all other ways of making a living; cultivation of the soil appeared slow by comparison with the hopes of a dealer. To "chop", or buy and resell at a profit, had an attraction that nothing could equal. Money made by dealing cost little in sweat; it was more an exercise of the wits than of the body.

Confirmed "dealers" would attend market regularly and would turn up at every sale in the locality. At market they were at hand to buy the disreputable pen of pigs or sheep that some self-respecting farmer was anxious to be rid of. The price was low; yet even when he was anxious to buy, the dealers' indifference to the auctioneer's request for a bid was an interesting study. The auctioneer knew his man; it was usually only a sly wink or a mere flicker of an eyelid that sealed the purchase. Dealers were careful not to risk much, often offering only the value of the skins, bones, and flesh as food for ducks and fowls. But there was always the *chance* of nursing the unhappy beasts back into health and condition; so those who bought them became experts on ailments; the animals in their care were almost as if they were in hospital, the rule "kill or cure" was so well observed.

Such people as these were never fearful of reputation, they were therefore open to act for farmers and dealers of stability, to sell for a commission a faulty beast that the owner preferred not to sell in his own name; or to buy from the flock the odd sheep that spoilt the appearance of the whole lot. In these ways they, too, seemed to serve a need of the countryside.

Joey (everybody called him Joey; in fact, he refused to be known by any other name) was a masoner; not highly skilled perhaps, but very handy at the repairs of farm walls or buildings; and as this was the kind of work undertaken by our firm I saw a good deal of him. He also knew about butchering, and reverted to that trade just before Christmas time, when little building work was doing. The butchers liked him, and had a long-seasoned joke to his credit, about some enormous amount of suet that he once claimed to have cut from a beast. At these times he appeared to be altogether one of the butcher fraternity, as he was at other times one with the masoners, who handled all that was concerned with lime and cement.

Joey was always happy at farm repairs, and especially when he was at work on the roof of a large barn or shed, repairing the tiling. If it was very cold, he had his joke at hand with him — "It wasn't no warmer on the roof", he would say, "although that much nearer to the sun." He perched himself comfortably on the slopes, taking out defective tiles and putting good ones in their places, or pointing the ridge or verges with cement; and he had his own little ditties that he sang while at work, pausing to call to his mate on the ground for more tiles, cement, or mortar. Whenever the repair work on a farm involved repairs to tiled roofs — and it usually did — Joey was the man deputed to the job. I am quite sure that he would have felt offended if the work had been given to anyone else.

So, too, with the cleaning out of a well or a sewage tank: Joey claimed to know them all, their size and capacity. He always groused at the job, yet was proud of his ability in handling them. To speak of a tank that he did not know, or had not at some time of his life cleaned out, would have been a reflection on him that the bravest did not dare to make. He often told unprintable tales of his experiences, and of wells and tanks long since gone out of use, all forgotten by mere ordinary folk who had not his professional knowledge.

Also, he was good at sweeping chimneys by the old method of a long rope with a gooseberry bush tied at its middle, the bush being pulled up and down the flues by one man at the top and another at the bottom. Of course Joey, with his fondness for heights, took the top end, where, happy amid the chimney pots, he would shout down the chimney to the man within to keep the doors and windows shut; this was to keep the soot from blowing up with the draught into his face. He boasted that no other system cleaned a chimney so well; and no one contradicted him in that.

As for building the *wichert* walls of the village, it seemed as though nature had shaped him specially for that job. His short stocky frame was just right for treading the material into a plastic mass; and when he was on the wall, building it with a wichert-fork, his shortness meant that he would not easily overbalance. Everybody knew when he was at wall building by the wichert that stuck to his boots, and the look of his clothes, which were of the same colour. Joey was quite content that they should; it was no mean experience to be able to look at a long length of wall, six to eight feet high, a wall good for centuries to come, and to know that he had built it all himself. One man for whom he was building a wall called him Nehemiah; Joey liked the compliment and often repeated it, but I doubt if he knew the reference.

In whitewashing he had great faith in a generous allowance of blue to his wash, especially when smoke stains wanted obscuring. The result was often pale blue; but nothing would convince *him* that it was not a good white. He also had his own favourite remedy for curing troublesome coppers that no one could make to draw well; which was to do away with the flue round the pan, and so arrange things that the heat passed direct to the chimney. Although coppers so treated needed a lot of fuel to heat the water, I never remember that anyone complained.

If the work lay at some out-of-the-way farm Joey revealed a special ability at night for making near cuts home. He had a sense of location and direction that enabled him to find ways in semi-darkness across ploughlands and marshy fields, ways that involved clambering through gaps in prickly hedges and risks of slipping into sodden ditches. Nothing would persuade him to keep to the road if a near cut offered. Your service to humanity was honourable, Joey! If I could meet you again I would pay for a pint, a seal of appreciation I know you would understand.

Squirrel, as everyone called him, was a native of the village too, though entirely free from the commonplace habits of normal village folk. He seemed to be simply a child of nature, happy in the open country, the rolling heath and the woodland. He knew not, nor desired to know, the ways of life and common comforts made dear to others by inherited tradition; he seemed to be still content to live as man may have lived long ago in days before such modern frailties of the flesh and spirit were known and adopted.

As soon as his baby legs could carry him, he ran the village green, that faces its venerable church, in the beauty of nakedness. It is true his mother was easygoing and was quite unconcerned at this early defiance of Victorian propriety, yet even she, when later years discovered no conventional wisdom in him, roundly declared that she would never have taken such pains to bring him up if she had known how he would turn out.

His proper name was William Smith, but the village, with its usual aptitude, knew him as "Squirrel", and by this name he lived and died. It seemed to us more suitable to an agile, carefree disposition and his happy-go-lucky life.

I never remember him to have been miserable, not even in the worst of weather or circumstance. He envied no man his higher fortunes, but lived in a state of natural joy, content amid pleasures to which he had some special right of access. A perpetual fount of humour bubbled forth out of his heart into quaint sayings. The village could not have done without him; for his sayings and doings were told with zest at almost every cheerful meeting.

He accepted none of the responsibilities of life, but took such remnants of necessity, in the form of food and clothing, as were given to him by those who would spare them. The result was that his body was well-nourished and his face smiling, though his clothes rarely, if ever, fitted; the sleeves of his jacket, and the legs of his trousers, were always either too short or too long, and lacking some buttons. Yet, in some way impossible to explain, he filled a place in the life of the old village, as no one else could have done.

His manner of speech was playful and peculiar, the notable trick of it being that he often reversed the order of the principal words of a statement. The sayings of Squirrel enriched us; he was even better known by his sayings than his doings. Should any villager push a wheelbarrow along the road, he would certainly be reminded by someone of Squirrel's famous saying that "nothing frightened a wheelbarrow like horses!" Let a man drive his ducks to the pond; as they joyfully took to the water, someone would say, quoting Squirrel, "Now they are landed!" Let him drive his horse and cart through the pond; sure enough, when he reached the other side safely someone would be handy with Squirrel's consolation, that now he was "safe in Old England again".

Squirrel seldom wandered far from the village, though once when he went with other men in search of harvest work at a distance, he swore "that he slept under a shock of corn and never had a wink all night". This hardly suggests that he was altogether careless of comfort as more normal folk understood the word. While his

141

parents lived a shakedown was always to be had at their cottage, though he did not always make use of it. Where he did sleep he alone knew; all that the village knew was that each day saw him shambling along its ways, happy and contented, his face suffused with smiles.

He had a ready word of consolation and cheer for those in distress. Once, watching a brewer's man unload a barrel of stout, he saw it suddenly slip endwise to the ground. Every joint of the barrel loosened with the jolt, and the rich brown stout was oozing from them all, forming a small stream, which flowed away down the dusty road. The poor drayman stood bewildered, not knowing what to do; but Squirrel, grasping the situation, danced round him, flinging his arms wide and shouting: "Can't be helped! Can't be helped!" — a useful drench from the well of Truth.

His service to the village was humble and invaluable. At that time the sanitation was very primitive; many cesspools — called *guzzle-holes* — and drains had to be cleansed every few days. No one wanted the job, so Squirrel undertook it with alacrity. It suited him very well, for it was quickly done; and it carried with it a hunch of bread, with a piece of cheese or the fag end of the family joint, and a pint of beer and sometimes even a copper or two with which he bought another. He had his regular round of calls. His cheery face would look in on the turmoil of domestic worry that buzzed in the scullery. There on a shelf he eyed the oddments from the larder waiting for him; the backyard was oftcn (as they called it) "clapered" with mud brought in on the boots of the men from the fields and roads — little use asking *them* to clean it away; they had promised times out of number and still it wasn't done.

Not so with Squirrel; he saw the need at once, and, like the Good Samaritan he was, took on the job without even being asked. There was the besom and the shovel; it was only a matter of his willing arms, and the yard was soon clean again. This was how he made for himself a warm corner in the heart of the mistress of the house. She, busy with her pots and pans, meantime listened to his cheery voice outside, his mutterings to himself, "Yard in a mess. Soon put it right." He knew that presently a horn of beer would appear through the doorway, and that another with food would be ready when the task was done. Not only that either; the housewife I am thinking of had an eye also on his poor old clothes; and Squirrel often went away with a jacket or a pair of trousers that she was secretly ashamed to see her husband wear again, although he himself had by no means left it off for good.

She believed with all her heart in thrift and work, and often said that she had no patience with idle folk and beggars. But this trait in her was counterbalanced by generosity to those who conformed to her way of thinking. She knew that she was reckoned hard and stingy by some, and was consoled by Squirrel's words to himself as he worked in her yard; "Very good oo-man", he would mutter.

Only sheer necessity drove Squirrel to simple begging; and even his begging was done with grace. At grandfather's door he once asked for a shirt. Kate, the housekeeper, said they had nothing to give away. "Then

I can't have nothing", he replied cheerfully, and walked away.

Threshing corn by the machine always needed extra labour, and farmers, at times, were hard pressed to find it. Squirrel was sometimes called in, and as the work only lasted one or two days, he did not object. Besides, beer was supplied at intervals. His particular job was to collect the chaff that fell out under the machine and to carry it off to a bay of the barn, a job that meant working in a cloud of dust from morning to night. There, in a mechanical blizzard, half blinded and half choked, eyes full, throat full, neck full of dust, Squirrel and others worked and sweated. There was no relaxation; the machine with its incessant hum set a pace, and never ceased to cast out the chaff, which had to be removed as fast as it accumulated. They spread large hessian sheets on the ground, raked the chaff on to it, and then, seizing the four corners, flung the whole bundle over the shoulder and carried it away. Barley was the biggest teaser; its beard had a rasp-like feel that specially irritated the nape of the neck and the back, and the workers were made acutely conscious of its presence on the spine, between the shoulders, and under the armpits. Yet amid all such minor discomfort Squirrel's cheerfulness was undaunted and supreme.

Once upon a time, when payment for a day's threshing was due to him, Squirrel walked all the way out to the far-distant farm to collect it, and found the farmer not at home. On going again the day following, he greeted the farmer with the name of his farm: "Good morning, Mr Stockwell Lane," he said, "I came to see you yesterday but you wasn't at home, so I thought I'd come and see you to-day, whether you was at home or not." The farmer tendered half a crown and a sixpenny piece. "No," said Squirrel firmly, "three equal shillings like other men, or nothing."

And once he lost his temper because of an infringement of what he regarded as a customary right. When the wandering instinct of youth had left him, he had attached himself to one certain farm, where he allotted himself a building with free supply of straw for his bed. But one evening when he came home to sleep he found that a load of roots had been tipped there. This was too much, even for *his* genial disposition; he rated the farmer for all he was worth; and the farmer to his credit and surprise, humbly apologized and promised that it should never happen again.

As he grew older, however, Squirrel sought out more comfortable quarters when winter came. He found them at *The Jolly Sailor* at a neighbouring town — a warm bed for a few coppers. In the twilights of late October when nipping winds chased the fallen leaves along the village streets, he could be seen shambling along towards *The Jolly Sailor*, cheery as ever. If it looked like rain, and you said you feared he would get wet, he would smile and shake his head and say, "No. If that rains I shall put on the brake, and run 'tween the drops!"

The way there led him past the historic village mill; this was his last place of call at night and his first on the following morning, and a meal was assured each time. He became a local agent for the miller, which suited both the miller and his customers. Squirrel never misconstrued or gave a bogus order. The villagers all understood his question: "Want anything sent?" Whatever it happened to be, barley meal, toppings, or poultry corn, it arrived the next day.

His calls came to be a proper part of the isolated life of the mill; his comings and goings and his cheery words were very welcome items in each day's routine. One evening he left in the usual way, heading fair for *The Jolly Sailor* across the intervening fields. When next day he did not appear, they were worried about his absence, and made a search for him. They found him dead beside a stream. The child of nature had ended his life in her embrace.

The parish buried him and the district mourned him, and no one since then has filled his place.

The village had its own ways of dealing with social offenders. The stocks had disappeared, but they were remembered by many, one of whom was my Sunday School teacher, carpenter on a gentleman's large farm nearby. He would illustrate the story of Paul and Silas, when that was our lesson, by telling us about the stocks that once were to be seen on the green alongside the churchyard wall. He was a kind old man, with sons of his own, grown to young men; and he understood the temperament of boys, and their interest in the history of their own neighbourhood. We never minded how far away he strayed from the subject proper; it was our delight to hear him tell how the drifts of standing corn were allotted to the faggers who had assembled to cut it; and the earlier methods adopted when it was cut by the sickle. Such tales made us feel that the village even then was getting hopelessly modern and up-to-date, especially when it came to the story, so often told, of the time when there was only one spring cart in the whole parish, its springs, too, made of wood. The shed where it was kept stood on my great-grandfather's farm, but I could never find out whether it belonged to him or not. But that was where it was kept, he said, and where people came to examine it for a novelty. And he always managed to bring us back to the lesson and to drive home some truth which we boys remembered all the better because of his easy teaching.

There was in the village a horn made of sheet copper, on which a deep, hoarse blast could be sounded; it was always hung on a certain thatched cottage home. In some unexplainable way it had come to be counted as village property, and was known to all as "the old speaking trumpet", or "the rough musicking horn".

If there was any notorious gross misbehaviour, such as the over-chastisement of a wife by her husband, or any other act not approved of by the village in general, its loud voice would be sounded in the quiet of an evening; and as soon as its rough music had died down, the noise of hobnailed boots would be heard pounding the village ways from all directions as the men hastened to the place of council.

There, a sack was stuffed with straw to represent the body of the culprit; a head, an old hat, and arms and legs made it into a gruesome guy, which was mounted on a hurdle and carried to the offender's house, followed by a rabble beating on old pots and pans. The noise went on while the guy was burned outside the house to disgrace the offender; and also, one must add, to delight the company, whose morals were often not much better.

Two of these rough musickings happened during my boyhood; and twice I remember how a young man was roped and taken to a pond and there ducked for being unkind to his parents. They told me that when he came to the edge of the water, he was philosopher enough to say: "If I have to go in, it shall be of my own free will", and straightaway walked out to the middle of the pond, where a pull at the rope threw him over.

But these were infrequent excitements in a village where the normal life was peaceable enough.

CHAPTER
TWELVE

George

This chapter is all about George the faithful, a man of character, like all other labourers, and one whose lovable disposition remains in fond remembrance, though his mound this long time has been green.

Of his long career of service, extending from childhood, I learned from his own lips at a time when, advanced in years and with the vigour of manhood almost gone, he became a father-instructor to me in my employ. I was then keeping two horses and the need for provender led me to take on a small holding of some twelve acres. George's long experience of land work, given to me without stint and with single eye to my interest, supplied the practical knowledge necessary for its cultivation. He was familiar with every detail of farming; able to lay a whitethorn hedge, to build and thatch a rick, or to thresh corn out with a flail, as once we had to do. He had, too, the rare ability of arranging the labour on the land at the right time and to the best advantage. That meant looking ahead and forecasting the needs of crops not yet planted, which, later on, would need attention.

He taught me how to broadcast seed corn on the bare fallow; he knew the proper width of stride from end to end; he taught me how to fling the handful of seed high and wide before me at every step, and that at the end I must turn and repeat the action on my way back. I was afraid that my inexperience would only give us an uneven crop, and I urged him to undertake the sowing himself. But he pleaded the stiffness in his limbs; with good reason, as I knew. For once, when I was following close behind him up a ladder, I heard an odd groaning sound, and when I asked what it was he told me that it came from his hip joints where, because of rheumatism, there was, he said, a lack of oil. The truth could not be denied; to carry a heavy *sidcut* full of corn, hooked to a leather belt round the waist, to steady it by grasping its handle with the left hand, and at the same time with each step forward to fling with the right a handful of corn, was beyond George's power, however willing of spirit he might be.

So he rigged me out and gave me careful instructions; and I was his willing pupil, and faithfully followed them. The experience had a quiet excitement for me; to sow seed by hand, in the crisp air of early March, was a reversion to primitive method such as suited my natural inclination towards things that were old. Certainly broadcasting of seed was a highly important part of ancient life before machinery had displaced man's labour, that change which has made work on the land seem so much more prosaic. But I was also conscious of delight in performing so crucial an intervention between man's need and nature's provision; and I believe all

150

know something of this feeling of ritual when sowing seeds in the springtide. I waited the growth of that crop with considerable doubt, but its evenness — equally spread all over the soil — surprised both myself and my neighbours, who all had much longer experience on the land, and had good reason to doubt my own skill. I felt proud of my first crop of broadcast oats; it had an interest, for me at least, entirely different from other crops planted by the horse drill.

George and I did not always agree, nor did I always take his advice without question; especially when, on planting potatoes, he urged that the premature shoot of a set ought to be rubbed off with the thumb before planting. He was convinced that the generative power was inside the tuber and that by some obscure process it pushed off the outside shoot. "To rub it away helps the potato", he declared, and, notwithstanding our many arguments about it, he died with the belief firmly in his mind. But if he was obstinately wrong about this, he was right about other things. Once when seed was scarce, he taught me — what seems a paradox — how both to plant and eat a potato. "Cut off the snout and give the rest to the missus for the pot", he said. "Just these bonny shoots and a little bit of flesh to feed 'um." He fetched out his hefty clasp knife — his entire cutlery outfit at mealtime — and cut off the ends, leaving more than three parts of the tuber for use in the home. "A little soot rubbed on the bare flesh will keep away the wireworm", he added. Just to prove if there should be any difference in the result, in comparison with those planted whole, we decided to mark the rows. But when we came to lift the crop, both of us had forgotten the divisions and could not see any difference in any part of the crop; it was all so even in result.

George was as observant as the village labourer generally is. He alone remembered the age of Old Betty, a venerable hen to whom had been granted the privilege of living for as long as she could. She was as old, he said, as my youngest child, who was then well advanced in her teens. Betty was a black Orpington, whose sprightly nature when she was young had saved her from the common fate of hens. And so she became a favourite whom no one felt inclined to eat. As time went on this sentimental reason for sparing her came to be supported by knowledge: each year (we knew) she grew tougher, and so at last she was simply allowed to live on, a life sedate and decorous.

Unheedful of the young gallants, the strutting cockerels and pullets brought to light and life by each succeeding year, Betty pursued her separate ways, alone from dawn till roosting time, seeking out the dainty morsel in odd out-of-the-way nooks and corners, where her advanced wisdom told her that certain titbits beloved of hens were likely to be found. She lived the well-ordered life; going to roost ahead of the others every night, and so making sure of her customary perch in the henhouse before it could be bagged by another hen. We all believed that she knew of her privileges, and even reflected on her experiences, so ancient and wise her life became by comparison with the brief life of other fowls.

Every harvest time she crossed the road and took up her temporary residence at the farm opposite, roosting each night on one of the farm carts in an open shed. For as long as the corn was being carted from the fields, she walked round and about the neighbouring ricks, picking up stray kernels of corn as long as they were plentiful. No one ever saw her return — it was like the coming and going of swallows and other birds in their natural state: a day came when Betty was back again in her familiar ways about the homestead.

No one knew how long she might have lived, had not her astonishing foresight contained the little flaw that led to her premature death. She was found dead at the farm opposite, with her crop packed full of soft new wheat, far too glutinous to pass through her gizzard. Some said that at her age she ought to have known better ; but I say it may have been her first experience of a damp harvest.

George (to come back to George!) taught me how to use a scythe. He arranged the correct hang or *pitch* of the blade to suit my height, and the most convenient position of the handles on the crooked stayl — called the *sned*. The paddock was not convenient for the use of a horse mower; every time we cut it for hay, scythes were produced for the job. On those days George arrived with his "mowing-belt", a dark leather band that had seen much service in years gone by. It had a worn, shining steel buckle at one end and elongated holes at the other. At the middle was a leather pouch for the "rubber". George said it was safest and wisest to keep the rubber always handy, to save unnecessary steps to find it when the scythe wanted sharpening.

I loved to see his bent form in graceful, rhythmical movement, swaying from right to left with supreme ease and skill. At his left hip the white stone rubber was poised in the pouch, as a kangaroo carries its young in its pocket. At each broad sweep of his scythe the sound of an otherwise inexpressible swish was heard, the noise of the sure severing of hundreds of minute stalks by the keen blade. They were gathered and carried to the left in billowy profusion, where they lay in a swathe ever lengthening. This was the poetry of perfect action; an old man in rough, worn clothes, transmuted, as I watched, by the artistry of toil.

The pathway left behind him was always of even width, clean cut from side to side; no strands of halm were left behind as tell-tales of imperfect skill, as my pathways. Sometimes it happened that the tall grass leaned all ways at once, making a clean cut difficult. George had his own name for those patches, "Bull's forehead", he called them.

My mowing was bungling by comparison. Ability like his demanded a long training beginning early, when the body was flexible and responsive. I found ligaments and sinews in opposition; every stroke asked an effort of the will. To George it was second nature. But he was sympathetic and patiently directed me. "You'll find it come easy when you gets used to it", he would say, as I mopped the sweat from my face. And indeed as time went on I did get a little better; but the experience only impressed me more with the skill of the land-worker, so little appreciated.

Our relationship was happy; an intercourse sweetened by admiration of each other's ability. He approached my woodcraft respectfully and did not hesitate to make me understand that he regarded the job of a carpenter as something far above that of a worker on the soil. But I had many a good reason to think differently. How easily, for example, how freely he used the whetstone — which he called the rubber — to give a keen edge to his scythe. How quick and crisp were those movements to each side of the blade alternately, at each strike the hard gritstone coursing its way along the delicate edge with melodious sound. So skilled in its use he was that he could strike freely to within a degree of his hand without incurring a cut. When a scythe was sharpened to his satisfaction he would sometimes hold the long gleaming steel to the light and bid me look at what he called "the dingle edge" — a myriad of tiny steel particles hanging all along the edge.

Words can never exactly express the *squish-skim* of the rubber running down that fine edge of steel. The movements were so swift, their contacts so precise! It seemed, and still seems, a contradiction of all the methods of tool sharpening to which a woodworker like myself has been accustomed. But no modern way has superseded it. The scythe and its whetstone are survivals; they have come down through the centuries unchanged in any essential, except, perhaps, that a manufactured stone is now largely used instead of the natural stone.

I am unable to say which was the more difficult to learn — the sharpening of the scythe or the using of it. It was only after much practice that I succeeded in giving a respectable edge. My strike with the rubber was so wrong at first that it did about as much harm as good to the delicate edge, and George had to come to my aid, time after time. A few swift deft movements, with the merry ring of the steel as it responded to the rubber, a satisfied glance at the edge with his experienced eyes, followed by an encouraging "Now try", was all that was needed. It was just as well we were alone together. Other witnesses might have humiliated me.

The little that I know about piling a load of hay on a cart, or building a rick, I learned of him. "You're the younger man, so you must go on the load and I'll tell you where to place it", he would say. After that the pitches came up to me with his directions. "Fore ladder", "Back ladder", "Hip-wad", "Binder", or "Fill up your middle", as he, from the ground, saw the need. As I placed the hay according to his directions the cart became hidden, and I, fork in hand, maintained my balance as well as I could on a rocking table of fragrant hay. "Keep your eye on the horse's head; it will give you the centre of the load", he would call up to me in his cheerful old voice; I can hear it now again, as I write.

He built the ricks, and explained his methods as I threw the pitches to him from off the cart. He showed how important it was to get a true corner to a square or oblong stack. The pitch of hay to form the angle was carefully placed well out in position; it seemed to overhang so much that I expected it to fall; but he said it must project like that to prevent the rain from the thatch soaking the sides of the rick. On the corner pitch he placed what he always called the *binder*, a pitch that gripped it half-way. The hay lifted by a fork was always called a *pitch*, and a convenient quantity for a pitch was sometimes called a *wad*. Each pitch was placed with judgement and method all round and over the rick, and the result was that the rick became one compact mass. Throughout the whole process of building the aim was always to keep the middle high. Such a rick would not suffer serious damage if a heavy shower should fall before it was finished. Also a high-built middle was essential for the convenience of the hay-cutter who later on must cut the rick for use.

The same principles applied to the cartage and stacking of corn; the sheaves were all to be placed to hold others in position. The land-workers were so familiar with these principles that they took no particular notice of them. To me, coming new to them, they were strikingly interesting; especially the methods by which the ears of corn were always protected by the sheaf that followed. I confess I was never able to build a square angle with the sheaves.

Once we found ourselves with no rough litter with which to make the base of a stack.

"I have built a plenty without", said George; and he did so then, first making a large shock with ears upward and leaning other sheaves aslant to it until the outside of the rick was reached. By that means no ears of corn were left in contact with the earth.

George thatched the ricks, both hay and corn, whilst I, his labourer, prepared the yolms of straw and carried them to him on the ladder. From the eaves to the ridge, each time to a width as far as he could reach — which he called a *stulch* — he arranged the straws evenly, ever overlapping those beneath. After combing them straight

157

and true, he fastened them with the straw bands that I had helped him to make, my contribution being the turning of the wimble, whilst he deftly gathered straws which he fed into the rope that lengthened from his hands as I walked backwards.

Only by working in common with the land-worker can his outlook on life be understood or his soul be known. To share his company at a meal under the hedgerow, through which his simple life and aspirations are revealed, is itself an education. He tells what he chooses of his life, with plenty of subtle humour. His listener learns that the primary joys are not to the widely travelled or to those who occupy the chief seats of state; and that nature has ever reserved not the least of her pleasures for those whose orbit throughout a long life may be within two or three parishes and the area of a few farms.

Often their task was solitary, in some far distant field, to which they would walk alone in the early hours and work alone all day, seeing no one to speak to perhaps till they got home in the evening. Such men learned much that is unknown to the ordinary person. The coming and going of the flock of rooks from the distant rookery, the position of the sun, the lengthening of the shadows, the condition of the atmosphere, each told them something of the day. Without a watch they knew the time to within a few minutes. When George smelt the engines on the distant railway he declared that it would rain before long. If I asked him when to expect it, he would reply: "Wait till the sun and the wind get together." And he was usually right.

If the primary needs were assured — food, clothing, and a small cottage — such men rarely asked anything beyond. The pity was that these were not always assured — that lives that asked so little should have been subject to fear that the little would not always be forthcoming. To them the old age pension scheme was like a godsend. George was always loyal to his class. A straggling flock of rooks haunted our village, "The allotment crows", he called them. "They live on poor men's crops", he said; "and when they're driven from one field of allotments they straightway fly off to another." George would never accept the modern view that rooks on the whole do more good than harm.

In religion the whole village was either church or chapel; there seemed to be no neutral attitude, perhaps because church and chapel were needed for marriage and burial, and so a neutral position, apart from higher matters, was plainly impracticable. George is buried in the churchyard; but in life he held himself to be definitely attached to the chapel although he did not attend regularly. Probably he passed through its Sunday School, and there learned what little he knew of reading and writing. He began work at nine years of age, as my grandfather did; nine was then the normal age for boys to begin. Praiseworthy efforts were made by Sunday Schools to teach reading and writing, so that, at least, the children might learn to read the Bible. But George made no "profession" (by which those in membership at the chapels were known); "That", he said, "he left to them better larned than himself". Yet there ever seemed to be in him the instinctive faith in an Eternal goodness in which poor folk such as himself had a share. Beyond that he was not disposed to go; he humbly regarded the ethics and precepts of religion as something above his understanding.

George was a survivor of the time when the weekly sermons at the chapels were almost all the news and education of the village, when newspapers were rare and other counteracting influences almost non-existent. To the preparation of these sermons much thought and study were given by worthy men of exemplary life and conduct, men whose influence cannot easily be over-stated. Such men were always at the forefront in matters of social progress, but even by them the far-reaching teaching of the New Testament had not then been fully grasped. The chapels, even, had their comfortable panelled pews for farmers and other better-off folk; the poor sat in meek humility on benches at the back. "Them at the front", one said, "has the first bite at what good comes from the pulpit and we have what they can't eat." "The rich man in his castle, the poor man at the gate" were accepted as rightly ordained conditions.

The merits of the weekly sermon were sometimes discussed at work in the fields. Monotonous tasks, such as hoeing roots, were livened up by friendly arguments about the preacher and the truths contained in his discourse. But George's interests lay more in the singing of the hymns. He had a good baritone voice, with a natural sense of harmony which enabled him to render his part with proper blend.

Hymns for places of worship; but anywhere else George's favourite song was *Life's a Bumper*. He often sang it as a duet with another native of equal ability. He always sang it at the annual allotment holders' supper. He was a general favourite; I never met anyone with a grudge against him. Courtesy was natural to him, though it may have developed when he was in gentleman's service, years before I knew him. He often spoke of a Mr Forthsythe, in the county of Berkshire, who had built his new house of soft white sandstone not far from the ancient city of Silchester. His most-told story of that time was related to the supply of beer to the workers. On the ground that it violated the licensing laws, an inspector in plain clothes had called at the office. But George recognized in time the regular stride of a policeman, and advised caution to Mr Forthsythe's son, who was in charge. The baffled policeman afterwards admitted that "it would have been a cop, if it hadn't a-bin for that jarvey".

George had even been a cab driver and was proud of his knowledge of London. He often boasted in his self-amused way of the time, late at night, when he was hailed by a toff:

"Hostler. Do you know London?"

"Yes, sir", George said he said.

"Then", said the young toff, "drive me to the first and last and the fifth day of the week."

"Right, sir. Jump in, please." This again from George. And — he continued, with his own grandiloquence — "I drove him straightway to *The Cradle and Coffin* in Friday street!"

"That was a knowing act on your part", said I, knowing by this time what was expected of me.

"Well, but of course I knew before", he confessed with delight. "There was the sign outside the pub, with the cradle and the coffin painted on it and the name, The First and Last, as I'd seen it many a time when driving down Friday Street."

Other anecdotes described life again in his native locality, where George and his wife lived in a cottage attached to a farm in a parish adjoining. To have a man close at hand was essential to the prosperity of this place, and the man had to be trustworthy and willing to get up in the night, to attend to the newly born pigs, calves, and colts, and their mothers. A position of trust exactly suited George's disposition; to him the master's interests were always his own.

George often told with pride of a record crop of potatoes he grew there for himself. He was given the use of a plot of land where a heap of mangold-wurzels had lately been removed. He did not say so, but I surmise that the residue from the wurzels was an ideal dressing for the crop. A long period of heat and drought succeeded the planting, and everybody's potatoes began to languish, so that crops were far below the average.

A rick of hay was built alongside George's plot. While it was building, the wind carried away from the elevator clouds of small shreds of dried grass, which settled lightly on the leaves and helm of George's crop until it was completely covered in with a light shield of hay. George's mates had a good laugh at its appearance. "But", said he, "I had the last laugh." For the potatoes thrived under the shade thus afforded, though no one knew they did till one Sunday morning, when his wife told him she had no more potatoes left in the house, and that he must go out and buy some. "I had my grave doubts," said George, "but I thought I'd try the plot." And every time he told the tale his eyes lit up at this point: "Such a crop," he would cry, "I could scarcely believe my eyes." "No buying potatoes for me!" he said, as he carried a boiling in triumph to his wife.

George's crop was the talk of the parish, for the potato was of unbelievable importance to the villagers in those days. They lived then so near to penury that, to George and his wife, a supply in abundance altogether altered the prospects of the oncoming winter, and coloured it with a cheerfulness that rang in his voice every time he told the story.

As long as George lived there, he was a welcome member of the community. He was not native, but he was amiable; everybody liked him.

It was a very old village of manor houses and farmsteads. Almost alone in its unabashed newness, a large Nonconformist chapel raised its red brick façade among them, its low-pitched slated roof in shocking contrast with the old roofs, gabled, lichened, and moss-grown.

Aesthetically the edifice was an ugly intrusion, discord in a harmony otherwise perfect. But the villagers saw it with other eyes; it was of good influence; it brightened their lives.

The church, in perfect lines of Gothic architecture, still witnessed to an earlier expression of the selfsame faith; but most of the villagers preferred the chapel. They did not mind so much about a lack of structural beauty;

it was nicely warmed in winter, the seats were comfortable, and people were welcome there. They worked hard all the week and it did not seem to matter to them that the service was not on classic lines. All they needed was exposition, simple and easily understood; and some joyous, sincere singing, in which they could all join.

The chapel had been built a generation or two earlier; it had meant much personal sacrifice, the memory of which remained a power. To maintain the chapel demanded the continuous self-denial that is essential to real allegiance; so that chapel folks felt themselves a live unity with a movement dependent on their own support. Parents had taken them to chapel as children; they had passed through its Sunday School, and to its influence indeed most of whatever was good in their lives could be traced. To many of them, throughout their lives, the chapel and its teaching represented the final expression of truth as far as they understood it.

George, speaking of what he remembered, often mentioned the large number of grey heads that could be counted in the seats each Sunday evening. To attend some place of worship regularly was then the normal habit of life. At the chapel they became familiar with all the recognized methods of delivering sermons and, though the substance of a discourse may often have been beyond their grasp, they were not slow to say whether or not the preacher had handled his subject well. The form of the sermon was something in itself. It was always interesting to note the separate heads taken up, each in its order, and each lucidly explained. If a point of special note was emphasized by a sharp rap on the reading desk, or a gesture of the preacher's hand, so much the better. Men who had worked the week through in the bleak fields felt drowsy in the cosy chapel, and some had fallen asleep and snored. Any sharp recall to duty was of acknowledged value.

George's intimate knowledge of that chapel life convinces me that he must have been a regular attender. Once at least he distinguished himself by making a miniature rick of corn with a ladder at its side, for part of Harvest Festival decoration. They liked it and honoured him by using it, but told him he ought to have painted the ladder red.

But the chapel (as George's memories showed) did not altogether escape the dissensions of democracy; differences of opinion now and then darkened for a time the underlying love and unity that were its strength. One of George's masters — a leader too — so strongly objected to some course decided upon, that he vowed he would never enter the chapel again "until he should be carried in". Time was the only healer. By and by those he had left missed him, and the old man himself also yearned to reoccupy his accustomed seat. But he had said what he had said; he was a man of his word, and could not go back on it. There was only one thing to do. Strong arms and willing hearts fetched a large chair, and he was carried through the doorway triumphantly.

During the second half of the nineteenth century a powerful crusade against drink entered the village. The chapel Minister gave his full allegiance to the principle of total abstinence. He knew full well that some folk

165

spent more on beer than they could afford, and that a few were sodden by excess. This could not be hidden, and was acknowledged; yet obstacles blocked the path of absolute reform beyond the power of its warmest advocate to remove.

The labourers' faith in beer was native; their stomachs were attuned to its flavour. It had been their drink from childhood, as it was also the drink of their fathers for generations before them. Life without it was such a novel idea to them that they flocked to the meetings to hear what was said against it. Nevertheless, some few went over to the new habit of life and suffered naught in health and rather the more gained in pocket; the majority satisfied their curiosity and kept to the old ways. It developed into a permanent controversy, conducted with a rare mixture of good humour and unceasing zeal. The abstainers in formation attacked the entrenched position of the barrels, across which their devotees maintained an unyielding resistance.

At the lectures it was easy to present the harrowing pictures of lives and homes ruined by excess. It was difficult, it was as good as impossible, to persuade any labourer that the pint he drank in the harvest field had no restorative virtue. There is a story of one such confession of faith which may as well come in at this place, though I did not hear it from George.

The lecture on total abstinence was ending, and the chairman, with commendable zeal for fair play, invited remarks from any who held contrary views. At once a tall and gaunt labourer rose to his feet, and said in a slow deep voice, that he had a few words to speak on the question. His peculiar disposition was well known and the audience anticipated some fun.

"I have been today", said he, "a-thatching a rick at Starvall farm. And when I was half-way up the ladder, all at once I come over so queer, as I could neither go up, neither could I come down. But I knowed very well what was the matter and what to do. So I shouts down to my boy who was on the ground a-making the yolms. 'Bono', I said, 'I must have some beer.' So Bono, he fetches me a quart, and I drank half a pint and felt a good deal better. Then I drank another half a pint and felt a good deal better. I drank the third half pint and then I felt all right. After that I went on and done a good day's work. You says: Beer ain't no good, but that's what it done for me to-day."

He forgot to say who drank the other half pint. With much hilarity the audience assumed that Bono himself had drunk it.

The Minister's vocation was itself his handicap. The labourers liked him as a man, friendly and with a pleasant word for all; they had no doubts whatever of the sincerity of his efforts for their welfare; but on the matter of beer, in the reserve of their own rural counsels they held him not equal to a sound opinion: "The man means well and believes all he says about beer being no good to nobody. But he's never done a day's real work, you know, not in all his life. If he'd had to pitch hay as I've done to-day, and be choked a-dry as I've been, he'd understand what a drop would do to help him along."

But as this opinion never came to the good man's ears he continued, in pulpit and out of it, to proclaim the wisdom of total abstinence. George, whether or not he accepted the teaching in principle, never put it into practice; and to *see* him drink a glass always seemed to do me good as much as it appeared to refresh him. In his stories of the controversy too, his loyalty to his own working class was again revealed. Because beer, the poor man's drink, seemed to be singled out from all other liquors for direct attack, they felt themselves subjected to unfair reflection. They said it was an injustice, and felt that it ought to be exposed.

They knew that though some farmers and other better-off folk had become abstainers for example's sake, others, on the quiet, still managed to keep a modest stock of whisky, wine, and whatnot besides, in the house. Nothing came up about this in the sermons, George said; "And I'd seen the bottles carried indoors from the cart when they came home from market. So I *know*", said he, with a nod of decision.

The grievance remained and grew, as grievances will. It came to a head as the time for the annual village feast drew near. From days far beyond the remembrance of the oldest man living, it had been a custom to have what they called "a skinful" at feast time. Until the bother about total abstinence nothing had disturbed the ancient celebration; it was as good as a customary right. But the abstainers had another opinion; and at the Sunday evening service preceding the feast the chapel Minister always preached what George called "a red fire-hot teetotal sermon", denouncing beer right hand and left.

George shared his fellows' sense of injustice. He felt it unfair to have to sit and hear the Poor Man's Drink condemned, with not a word said against tipple they could not afford. It needed definite action. In the back of his own mind he planned a scheme in which he — the valiant — would champion the rights of all his fellows. He outlined his plan to them; but they were sceptical and, though everyone knew that the men of George's native village were rare ones for radical pluck, they doubted his courage to carry it through.

But George's strength lay in his native courtesy. No one else had that easy approach, or his good-tempered way of stating a case and so gaining a sympathetic hearing. This he knew; "Leave the matter in my hands", he said with assurance; and they were modest and were only too glad to do so.

The act was timed for the following Tuesday afternoon, when the chapel Minister made his weekly visitation at the farm where George lived and worked. At that particular time it might have happened that the men were all working in some far-away field. But fortune blessed them; George and his fellows were busy repairing hurdles in the very shed next to his cottage. Nothing could have been better. "Now", said George; "when he comes, he will first call on the mistress, and then go in to have a few words with my wife. I shall follow him, and, what's more, I'll leave the door open so that you can all hear exactly what I say to him."

The Minister came to time, and did just as George said he would. Seeing him safely enter, George laid down his tools and went in. When George told me this story, as he often did, his manner hinted that the destiny of an empire rested on the issue.

"I want to be so bold as to ask of you a favour, sir", said George.

"Certainly, George. If it's anything in my power, I shall be only too glad to do it."

"As I expected you to say, sir", replied George. Then he paused, to give weight and emphasis to what was to follow.

"You know, sir, as how next week is the feast; and I expect, as you have always done before, that next Sunday evening you'll preach a teetotal sermon."

The Minister waited. George was treading on delicate ground, but his genial manner carried him over where many a one would have floundered.

"Very likely", said the Minister at length. "In fact I've made some notes already."

George gave his head a slight shake. "Not that I would go so far as to ask you not to preach it; not that at all, sir; I would like you to understand that."

"Certainly, George, certainly."

"What I wants to ask you, sir, is a favour to us working men: that this time you take for your text, Whisky, Rum, and Brandy. I am not going to tell you how to deal with them, for that you understand far better than I can tell you. We shall be well satisfied whichever way you place them. You can make Whisky, or Rum, or Brandy your first head, and bring the other two in just as you think best. It matters not to us, so long that you stick to them three and leave beer alone for once. For, you know sir" (impressively) "the beer is the poor man's drink, and only them as can afford it have the Whisky, and the Rum, and the Brandy."

"Whatever did he say to that?" I would ask at the end of the story. "He was obliged to laugh, you know", said George. "He said that there was no such text in all Scripture. But he promised that he would consider it, and there we left it."

The news spread like wildfire all over the village. Everyone was talking about it, and saying that the Minister had promised to preach on Whisky, Rum, and Brandy the next Sunday evening, that he was going to take them for his text. And everyone vowed they would go and hear what he said.

"Was it a big congregation?" I asked.

"Big! I should think it was, too", replied George, chuckling at the remembrance. "The chapel was packed; every seat was full, gallery and all. I forget the text he preached from but it was something about strong drink, which he denounced right hand and left, for all he was worth. And we sat there drinking in every word he said; and though he did let fly, and made remarks so that we could all know what he was hitting at, the word *Beer* was never mentioned from beginning to end of his sermon."

"I was the hero of the day", he proudly added. "I could have swam in beer; everybody wanted to treat me. And how I got up into the clubroom I never shall know, for they carried me up the stairs."

Though George's description of the feast itself was brief, he made it clear enough that the time-honoured method of celebration was honoured once more, and that his own condition was nothing short of a "skinful". To him, as to others of the old school, the feast was plainly a pleasant interlude in a life of almost perpetual toil.

Kind justice demands that we should see it from that end, and that we should note the almost entire absence of influences that have fashioned our own lives on rather different lines. To drink as much as possible, when opportunity offered, was to George the undeniable right of the working man. He saw these things as they had been seen in former days and conditions: his appetite had never known the variety (not to say luxury) that now appears on our tables. If we must regard his excesses as a failing, I am glad to know and to bear witness that it was more than counterbalanced by the remarkable virtues of his simple character.

CHAPTER
THIRTEEN

The Life of the Boy

Men of my age have often said that boys don't seem to enjoy life with the zest that we knew when we were young. We remember our rollicking ways; we remember that life abounded with interest and delight, and that we were determined to enjoy every moment of it. We remember a carefree existence, when each season brought its own opportunities and its own delights, which coloured all its hours, sunny or drear alike.

The village school taught us our lessons, but left us free to arrange our own amusements outside. These were either of our own invention, or else traditional games that our fathers and grandfathers had played years before. I daresay we enjoyed them all the more because they were not provided for us. Most of us had also read books about some sort of "Desert Island", and we longed (as others have) to be stranded on one, where the ignominy of school and all such irksome duties would be unknown. There was no desert island near at hand, but we found the next best thing in the fields and lanes of the parish, and its stream and ponds, few of which are not still associated with some adventure of our youth.

The village school united us. We all suffered it, we all endured it, we all resented it, and we were agreed at least in our dislike of its bondage. No one expected us to *like* school; indeed, the adult idea was that it was good for us to be made to do what we didn't like. Not until I had passed my teens did the notion that school might be attractive ever enter my head. Then the chance reading of an inspector's report, where the lack of pictures, or flowers, or anything else of grace or beauty was commented upon, suddenly revealed to me a new outlook on child-life only then being slowly accepted.

My schoolmaster got his appointment just about the time when I began to go to school, and his career in our school lasted until just after I left. A more sincere or better-meant man could not be imagined; he was active in all social movements for the good of the village; but as head of its school no one could have called him a success. The number of children passing the yearly examination dropped to about one-third of the whole school, and as the financial aid granted by Authority depended directly upon examination results, matters became serious for the ratepayers.

The board of management was divided; half the members were Nonconformists who liked the master for his general character, and the other half were farmers who were not enthusiasts on any kind of education; and between the two he kept his post. But about the time I left school the radical element contested the election, urging the village to "Vote for the New Board! Efficiency with Economy." Only one of the old members survived this election, and under the new management the master resigned.

The school day varied little. Every morning at nine o'clock (after a run in the playground, where on cold days "cockwarning" was a favourite game) we were rung into the school room by a bell on the roof. We sang the morning hymn ("Awake, my soul") led by a bronchial harmonium, which one of the monitors played. I do not remember ever singing another opening hymn; we never expected to, and the idea seems never to have occurred to those in control. When I was moved up from the infant room, I picked up the words as well as I could, from others who had picked them up before me. None of us knew the right wording, and most of the hymn was sung to an incredible jargon in which only a few lines were rendered fairly correctly. Outside we compared our versions, which were always different, except that all agreed in singing "Shake off dolls' clothes" as the third line of the first verse.

An extempore prayer by the master followed; and then he mounted his platform desk and filled up the register, while we were given a lesson from the Old Testament by a monitor, who read aloud the vivid records out of the Books of Joshua, Judges, Samuel, and Kings. Those readings were anything but dull to us; we took the side of the Israelites, regretted their reverses and revelled in their slaughter of the Amalekites and the Jebusites, wicked tribes who deserved to be swept off the face of the land to make room for the chosen people of God. Now and then the monitor stopped and questioned us; those whose answers were wrong were called from their seats to stand in line at the front, along with any others who had otherwise misbehaved.

All through that scripture lesson the master was peaceably at his own duties — we noticed that he would spend much time every day in sharpening his pencil to a good point. But the quiet buzz of work was once suddenly broken when a screaming boy burst open the outer door, with his angry mother at his heels shrieking upon him: "Go to school! Go to school!" all the while belabouring him on the back with a leathern belt. She had thrashed him along the village street; now she thrashed him all round the room, and afterwards explained her mission to the master, who, more than a little surprised, had left his pencil and come down from his desk.

When the scripture lesson was over he caned all the boys (and now and then a girl) who were standing out in line. One strike across the fingers of the outstretched hand was the normal allowance; he seized the ends of the fingers with his left hand and gave the strike with his right. When the row of culprits was extra long, he began normally, but increased in zest as he proceeded, so that the poor unfortunates at the end could not keep back the tears. To be beaten without weeping was our ideal; we used to time how long the tingling lasted by the clock on the wall, and compare times later to know who had endured the most. We all believed that a horse-hair wound round the fingers would split the cane; one boy once attempted to test the belief; but the master saw the horsehair and gave him an extra allowance.

Arithmetic followed scripture, and then we went out to play. Writing and reading were taken in turn. One lesson each week (the last half-hour on a Friday) was devoted to drawing. I liked drawing most of all and wished that it were longer and more frequent. I liked history and geography too; but we had little at the best of times and for a period we had none at all; but in grammar, which I liked least, we were trained incessantly. I have a hazy memory of taking sentences in hand, and of tackling each word in turn, declaring parts of speech, person, number, gender, and case. I was always weak on cases; but as "nominative" seemed to be most frequent, I got into the way of using it in all my answers, until the master found me out and saved up for me the words that were not in the nominative case. Only because I know now that children can learn anything am I able to understand how it was that we could gabble it off as we did; but how grammar was an aid to speaking or writing nobody had the faintest idea, then, and nobody has been able to advise me since. On leaving school I straightway forgot it all, as all the others did.

The schoolmaster had many claims on his time from village activities outside the school. When he was called away he left the school in the charge of his wife and the monitors. Those days were their terror and our disorderly delight. He was a keen total abstinence man; and the hymns for our singing lessons were all out of the "Band of Hope" book. The Inspector was a captain of the local volunteers. I have a vivid remembrance of his cynical expression as we sang to him, "I love the merry rill as it rushes down the hill" at the yearly examination.

One spring *Tom Brown's Schooldays* gave us all the idea of paper-chasing. We filled two bags with paper shreds ready and eager for the next holiday. Fortune quickly favoured us; a few days afterwards we were unexpectedly disbanded for the whole day. Joyous shouts of "paper-chasing" instantly arose. I was chosen to be one of the hares; and we slung the bags over our shoulders ready for the chase.

They said they would give us a start of ten minutes; but no watch was at hand, or monitor to rule. We started off; but before we had got more than half a mile away we looked back, and saw to our dismay the whole pack of hounds careering after us. We pulled ourselves together and ran and ran, but they were gaining ground on us. We were already breathless and felt near to exhaustion; though the hounds seemed to have plenty of wind and were coming stronger than ever. The thought of being caught so quickly only two miles from home was unbearable; there was nothing for it but strategy. A curve in the road favoured us; we tumbled over a field gate and lay flat in a ditch under a whitethorn hedge; we heard the noise of many feet pass and disappear in the distance. We had recovered our wind, however, and now took a short cut over the field and joined a path that ran parallel to the road. After another mile they sighted us again from another gateway, but a comfortable distance away.

Pell-mell, over the gate they came and the chase was in full cry again; we ran along a deep green lane and on into the little hamlet of Owlswick. There we heard shouts from behind, the voices of our pursuers crying breathlessly: "We don't want to run any further!"

So the chase ended and the day began again, as it was bound to do for a gang of happy boys, four miles from school, with a delightful May day at their disposal. Dinner was mentioned; we decided to go without dinner;

each boy was hungry but declared he didn't mind. It was of course a heroism to go without. So we meandered about the fields, the hedges, and the lanes until, at three in the afternoon, we were within a mile of home.

There were tall elm trees near by, with trunks straight as factory chimneys and nests of cawing rooks on the top. We paused and boasted a little. But one and all knew that to climb and reach them was impossible; we imagined we might perhaps have reached the branches, but the nests were all at the ends of slender twigs, where no one could possibly come at them.

Only a mile a-field, said one of the boys, there was a rookery where the nests were on branches low enough to be reached. Dinnerless and now so near home, nevertheless we all decided to go on. The way was over lonely fields, and the rookery stood near to an old moated enclosure, where formerly an important homestead had stood. There were the trees, tall elms with many nests, and one nest on a low, slanting branch. One boy climbed up, but when he found he could not reach the nest, he poked it from beneath with a stick, and a young, half-fledged rook — we called it a "calabolcher" — fell flop to the ground. We carried the calabolcher home in triumph, a fine memento of a glorious day, and somebody's mother made a dumpling with it.

We finally reached our homes at six o'clock in the evening, hungry as hunters, having tasted nothing but the water of the streams since far-away breakfast-time.

My brother and I were lucky to have the sons of a farmer as playmates. He allowed us the run of his farm, where there was a great deal of fun to be had the whole year round from its fields, its streams, its ricks and barns. We fished for roach and crayfish in the streams; to catch the crayfish we stripped halfnaked and put our hands into the holes of the banks, where they lay head outwards, with one pinching claw on each side. Then we slipped our fingers behind the crayfish and drew out each creature quickly and threw them to the bank to be picked up by one who carried a basket. On one memorable Saturday we came home with sixteen dozen and four. Our parents objected at this; they had had experience already — not unlike the plagues of Egypt — of crayfish crawling all over the house; and we had to take them all back.

Rat-catching in the wheat ricks was arranged for Saturday afternoons, when an old blind rat-catcher arrived, led by another who carried a box of ferrets. The ferrets were put into the holes in the ricks, and a stampede of rats quickly followed, flying from the ricks on all sides, to be caught and killed by the waiting dogs outside. The old man handled those ferrets with great care and knowledge. If a stubborn rat sat tight at the end of a hole, the rat-catcher would try one ferret after another before he was able to dislodge it. The successful ferret would grip the rat, and the rat-catcher would pull on the hindquarters of the ferret; sometimes every ferret failed until he tried his proven favourite.

When the weather was moist and there was nothing better to do, we played at war in a grass field where two dykes lay, which we used as camps. Each side claimed a dyke and made a stock of soft mud balls; these were our artillery; each side pelted the other.

Our battles began with Goliath challenges shouted from one leader to another. These were followed by volleys of mud balls. It was not difficult to dodge those thrown high in the air, but one thrower (I was always anxious to be on his side) had a way of throwing them with level, deadly accuracy about a yard above the ground. There seemed no way of escaping his swift and decisive aim; the only thing to do was to turn and take the blow on the largest, most convenient, and least vulnerable part of the body.

Marbles were popular when the roads were dry enough. All the village shops had them for sale: large glass Alley taws, with a coloured spiral cage within the glass; commoners, brown, blue and green, made of real marble rolled round and coloured afterwards; and a cheaper kind, called codlins.

Skill at marbles seemed to be more a matter of strength of muscle than anything else — the power of the thumb to shoot the Alley from the knuckle and to knock the marbles out of the ring. I was very fond of the game but was never very good at it. I found it difficult not to believe that certain Alleys had some special quality of their own, and that success was as much in owning a good Alley as in being a good player. Every boy of those days had marbles in his pocket somewhere.

A more hurly-burly game that we sometimes played was called "ducks". It was played with the large stones with which the roads were repaired. The game had its rules — all good established games must have rules — and though they were old they were simple. Each player chose a large stone or "duck" for himself; two other stones were set up one on the other in the middle of the road, and one player, the "duckman", placed his stone on the top of these two. Others threw their own ducks at the stones in position. If they knocked them down, the duckman had to put them back, but if their stones fell short of the line drawn across the road, he had the right to touch them (saying "tig") as the player ran forward to get them back.

No one wanted to be "duckman". He was up against all the others, and often when he had made a "catch" he found some other player had knocked the central stones down; and a catch in this event didn't count. It was a simple game, but we had great fun with it. To remember a game of ducks is to remember a great deal of laughter.

The girls played a quieter game. They made cup-like holes in the turf of the green, where they put coloured snail shells ("oddys", or "oddy shells") found in the hedgerows. Each in turn rolled a large Alley up to the holes, and when it settled in one, they won the oddys that it contained.

Life was happy in those, now far-off days, even when no telephone wire had penetrated the village, and no swift express train had sped by. We never expected to see vehicles run without horses, or planes fly overhead. It was excitement enough to mount a "bone-shaker" and ride as fast as six miles an hour, and to boast that when we got a bit older we would be able to take on the high cycles — now called "penny-farthings" — that had just appeared. But at least, the simple games we played developed our bodily powers and fitted us for the manual work that awaited us all.

My father believed in education, and had sent my elder brother to a secondary school at the town nearby. But he seemed to get so little good of it that father decided it was not worth the cost. The only visible result of his schooling that I remember was the "Psalm of Life" in copper-plate penmanship on a large sheet of mill-board, for which 2*s*. 6*d*. was added to father's bill. He was disgusted, and I was fed-up about hearing about it, so, at thirteen and a half, I kicked the dust of school from my feet and gaily entered the other school of manual activity.

CHAPTER
FOURTEEN

Father's Ponies

Not that father was a horsey man; but he liked to keep a pony for business and family purposes. Tommy, the first one that I remember, was said to be thirty years old when he died. As that happened when I was about ten, only the latter part of his life came into my experience.

We children, brothers and sisters alike, regarded so old a pony with the veneration that youth gives to age and experience. When he was not at work, he browsed the days away in our orchard, where we also played. He endured our patronage and torments with mute toleration, save once, when a well-placed and well-deserved kick caught me full on the hip, to remind me that there were limits even to Tommy's endurance. We felt sure that he regarded himself as part of the business and family institution; beyond this we could not read the workings of the mind behind that shaggy forelock and those luminous eyes. But nothing seemed more certain than that, whatever ideas of dash and speed he may have had earlier in life, they had all been discarded long since, and that Tommy's conscious desire now was to take life as easily as possible.

By continuous urgings, with now and then a reminder of a whip, Tommy could just be persuaded in harness to a steady jog-trot. Speed did not really matter much in those days; yet we were always wishing that his gait was quicker, especially on the rare occasions when someone was going a journey by rail, and the drive to the chosen station would be three, five, or seven miles. But as no one carried a watch, everyone was afraid of losing the train, and we were all so careful to allow plenty of time for the journey that we invariably found ourselves with half an hour to spare when finally we reached the station. When driving Tommy about the village we children could not help noticing how the smart butcher boys dashed by us, with their superior poise and withering glances of scorn at our old steed. Tommy did not mind them. He seemed to have given up all ideas of "going one better than your neighbour", if he was ever prone to that folly.

Out of sixty vanished years a general remembrance of childhood's bliss rises now; my brother and I are seated on the floor of the cart, our heads no more than level with the openings of its sides, riding eagerly along through a sunlit countryside. Father and mother are on the seat in front of us; their homely conversation mixed up with that constant advice and command to the reluctant Tommy, that was necessary to keep him going along at his usual jog-trot. Whenever it changed over to a slow walk we boys behind burned to know the cause; often it was nothing but a trail of newly deposited droppings on the road; the right to walk on such occasions was allowed; and Tommy knew as much and sometimes assumed the need when it did not exist, for which he was called an impostor. Those "slowing downs" were delightful variations of the ride. At times it was a stretch of newly scattered flints, and then we took the side of the road, one wheel travelling on the flints while the other skirted the grass verge. Then it was fine fun, for the cart was on the slant, and the child on the high side had all he could do to keep from sliding on to the other. There were also joyous bumps when the wheel went over the large flints as Tommy dragged the cart along. Other hindrances were equally interesting to us; the large flock of sheep tended by a sunburned shepherd and a yelping dog; or a large farm wagon drawn by two big horses, taking up altogether so big a share of the road that we turned to the side until one wheel bumped into the channels that the roadman had cut to let the water off the road. Everyone of course greeted father in passing and had something to say about the weather. We felt grateful that he was so well known and liked.

Those rides out with father took us to places far more rural even than our native village; isolated farms reached by crossing fields and opening several gates; small obscure villages, whose folk stared with curiosity, so rarely did they hear the sound of an unknown vehicle. In one village I always noticed that faces would peer through the lattice windows, or the doors would open slightly as we passed the cottages in succession. At times our return home would be in darkness too thick for us to see the road at all. Lights were not compulsory, and father held the opinion that they confused rather than helped a horse. And it is true enough that Tommy never failed to get us home safely without them; and often the choice of the way was left entirely to his discretion. In the darkness we knew when another cart approached by the noise it made; then father would shout and turn off with one wheel well on the grass verge until we had passed, which we also knew mainly by sound. In rain and snow we all sat tight together underneath a large gig umbrella that shed tears on those sitting outermost. A head wind at such times made driving pretty difficult; if you held the umbrella forward it impeded the sight, which worried the one who held the reins, and made him keep on asking that it should be held just high enough for him to see underneath.

Once, going to a market town nearby, we passed through a toll gate that must have disappeared soon afterwards, for I have no other remembrance of it. Father paid threepence for it to be opened, but no charge was made on our return.

Only once was Tommy known to run away, and that was when out of harness, and in the dead of a windy night when all the village was aroused and a windmill was blazing furiously. Tommy was madly excited at the unexpected glow and clamour, and when father — who had left his warm bed — opened the orchard gate to go out, Tommy rushed out before him, and careered about the village at a gallop. Father spent the rest of the night searching for him, so not until the following morning — when I went with him — did he see the burning mill, by that time nothing but a pile of blazing timber.

One act of insubordination is also recorded against Tommy, when father attempted a short cut over some fields which involved fording a shallow stream. Tommy saw the reflection of himself in the water and refused to cross, and father had to go round by a way three times as long.

I have a gruesome remembrance of his once being led home with each fore knee a slither of blood. He had fallen down at a sharp turn in one of the village ways; and he could never be persuaded to trot round that particular corner afterwards.

His reputation outlasted his life by several years. The saddler who took him in hand after death found his hide to be of extraordinary toughness; so he cut it up into bootlaces which he sold to the village workmen. Their reputation was prodigious. Never before or since (the saying was) were such laces known.

The story of father's next pony begins before he belonged to us. We had moved to another house, and our new neighbours, expecting a boy to stay with them, suggested that he might play with us. They offered the free use of a pony belonging to the village store. We liked the idea and agreed to it. The pony had been a favourite and had lived idly in a stable ever since its work had been taken over by a younger and faster horse. It had been idle so long and had become so fat with good food and idleness, that many declared it would never be willing to work again. They were wrong, however, for it willingly carried as many boys as could sit astride its fat back wherever they wished to go, and also — as you shall hear — gave one exhibition of excessive speed.

We rode it daily while the boy remained in the village, and father himself inclined to it with increasing favour. He wanted a pony, and considered it steady enough for his purpose. At length he asked the price, and being offered it at five pounds, bought it at that sum, and found himself held in derision by at least half the village folk.

Any sale of a horse was then a matter of public interest on which almost everybody expressed an opinion. Many people were so concerned, that they would resort to a place where beer was sold, though they might have no actual interest in the deal, to discuss its merits. Further, there was a kind of unwritten law about the way such sales ought to be conducted; and father had violated this. In all the long history of the village no one had ever been known to pay the price actually asked, without trying to get a bit knocked off. It was father's way always to ask what he expected to take, and he believed that others should do the same.

But those who had to do with horses had their own way of conducting a sale. Before any mention of price was made, everyone went to a house of refreshment so that the mental barometer should rise to a favourable point. Then an offer was made and a bid was named, the one high and the other low, each knowing that when the deal closed the price would be about midway between. In the intervals of bargaining everyone came out while the horse was run up and down the street amid shoutings and sharp flackings of whips, like miniature guns going off. Often the struggle was a long-drawn-out one, needing much libation to close it. Father's method was by comparison humdrum to the extreme.

The pony's name was Pedro. Mother mistook and called it "Pruno", and the mistake became its new name for us. Pruno's attitude to life was so like Tommy's that no more need be said. I will tell only one story of Pruno.

It was held to be a boy's job to harness the pony in a cart, and so whenever my sisters wanted Pruno, they claimed the right to ask us to do it. One day my brother was sent to fetch the pony from a paddock a quarter of a mile away. He brought it home by the forelock, because he could not find the bridle. Nobody else could find the bridle at once, and there was some fuss about the delay.

It was my own idea, to get matters forward, that I would harness the pony in the cart and put the bridle on when it was found. I soon had Pruno, docile as a lamb, safely between the shafts, with all attachments made except the bridle. As he was very fond of the grass on the other side of the road, I thought it no harm that he should have a bite whilst waiting. Now bridles, as I knew, have blinkers, flat pads of leather on each side over the eyes. I had asked father what they were for and he told me that they prevented a horse from seeing anything at the side of the road that might frighten it. At school they were far too keen on teaching us grammar ever to mention the purpose of a horse's harness; so I had to learn by experience, and this was going to be the occasion.

I moved Pruno a few paces forward and then gave him a free head to go to his beloved grass, as we had always done before. Instead, he turned his head and looked behind to see — what I learned he had never known before — that a cart with two wheels was following him. He gave a jump forward; the cart jumped too; the jump changed to a trot; the trot to a gallop, until, terrified, the old pony charged at terrific speed over a long stretch of grass (where now stands a Coronation Seat) heading straight for the village store.

In vain I ran, shouting to him to stop; Pruno had no other heed than to flee from the cart that chased his heels. Beyond the store a low garden wall projected; in a moment, as I saw, he would crash on this wall. But, just in the nick of time, and though terribly affrighted at the cart behind him, he saw the danger only a few yards ahead. Well on the cobble path in front of the store, he placed his four legs rigidly to stop. But the impetus was too great; he slid the whole length of the cobbles, and then missed, by a miraculous swerve, the projecting angle of the garden wall, which came in for no more than a blow from the hub of the cart wheel as it passed.

That checked the speed, and before he was well started off again a sprightly young man (who had been watching the blacksmith shoeing horses at the forge opposite) ran forward, held his stick in front of the pony's eyes, and at the same time shouted one sharp, decisive "Whoa!"

And Pruno came to a dead stop, with every muscle on the quiver. The young man seized his head, the villagers gathered round, everyone came out of the store and the blacksmith's shop.

"He hasn't got his bridle on", shouted one.

"Put his bridle on", said another.

My brother had just come along carrying it in his hand; mother also, terribly agitated.

"Here is the bridle", said she: "let the poor thing have it on." Someone put it on the pony's head. All its terror subsided at once; and no one understood why it had been harnessed without it.

My sisters had their drive after all, and to me remained the duty of going to tell father all about the mishap.

"It has only knocked one little piece of brick off the wall", I said.

He looked very grave; left his work, and went with me to inspect the damage. We found that the proprietor of the store — Pruno's former owner — was enthusiastic. He had seen it all. "Never" — he said with emphasis — "never could I have believed that my old pony could run so fast."

Father gave a local bricklayer sixpence to make the damage good. No one, save myself, now knows the story of that little patch of cement.

Father had four ponies in all. The one that succeeded Pruno was, I always felt, the most sensible of the lot. It was not too old, was sandy-coloured like the original Tommy and was therefore given the same name. It was fairly large and stocky in build; just the type of pony for hauling a moderate load about; it was like those satisfactory people who simply do what is expected of them and make no fuss about it. A relative who understood horseflesh bought it for father, the price being somewhere about ten or twelve pounds. Father grew fond of it, and, although when it got too old he bought another to help us in the work, he kept it going until after he had retired from business. It had a paddock to itself, where one Sunday afternoon my infant daughter and I found it dead. I had not the heart to tell him, so led the child forward instead.

"Tell Grandpa", said I.

"Poor Tommy, poor Tommy, dead", prattled she. He made no answer, yet I saw that he was moved, as those will understand whose contact with an animal has developed an affection that cannot be explained by words.

Number four, the only pony that father sold alive, was a fast goer, with an action that was the admiration of horsey folk. We liked driving it because it covered the ground quickly, but in fact it was not the ideal pony for quiet-going folk like ourselves. Also it had some peculiar habits, one of which was, when being unharnessed, to dash out of the shafts before the last attachment had been released. After several narrow escapes, we learned the wisdom of tying its head to a tree and pushing the cart away, instead of allowing the pony to walk out of the shafts. It also had an aversion to the steam traction engines that trundled about the roads at that time.

An uncle from town visited us. I met him off the train at a distant station, and on our drive home he lectured me on the management of horses. At the end of his visit I started him off, with mother and two others (one an invalid) — two in front and two behind — to drive himself to the station. After they had left I had occasion to cycle up the village, where, to my dismay, I saw them ahead with a traction engine approaching. My feelings were relieved when I saw uncle dismount to lead the pony by. But he improved the occasion by pausing opposite the engine — which had stopped — to give the pony a lesson. Turning its head towards the engine, he said, "There now, it's nothing to be afraid of!" But the pony, who understood being led by, did not understand being expected to stop and look at the engine, the escaping steam from which was making a sizzling noise.

Uncle did not know that it was unwise to give such a lesson with people in the cart, or that he ought to have kept at the front of the horse's head and not at the side. The pony made a dash forward; uncle, hanging on at the side, pulled it towards the ditch, where the shaft of the cart pushed him further until he fell in amongst the nettles. That released his hold on the pony's head and enabled mother, who held the reins, to pull into the road; but I, speeding up on my cycle in alarm, saw the wheel almost in the ditch and expected to see the cart go over.

Uncle was a big man, but I imagine he felt small when he got up out of that ditch. At any rate, he gave me no more lectures on the management of ponies.

CHAPTER
FIFTEEN

Some Old Customs;
Mummers and Maydays

The Village Feast

No institution was more popular, or more deeply rooted in village sentiment, than our annual Feast, which fell on the first Sunday after the nineteenth of September, and was always celebrated on the following day.

The observance seemed to be as old as the village itself, as possibly it was, for some said it was originally held in honour of the patron saint of the church, St Mary. No record remains to show whether or not the church began it, or in what manner she celebrated it; we only know that the village always honoured the Feast with a zest that it brought to no other event.

This may be partly explained by the scarcity of holidays — my father frequently said that at the time of his youth two holidays only each year were recognized — Christmas Day and the Feast.

Beyond that, it should be remembered that as lack of plenty to eat was the normal experience of the poor a century ago, so a day given to fill the belly with good food was a delight. Inquiries of old folk show that the ancient celebration was really of that character, a literal feast of good food and drink, with the mirth that goes with these things. Long rows of stalls were put up, where every kind of delicacy to tempt the appetite was displayed, sausages, cakes and sweets, baked pears and nuts, and all for sale. These were managed by folk of the village. One stall-keeper (so George said), finding his supply running short at mid-day, walked to the town six and a half miles away and came back with a large basketful for evening sale.

For the feast did not then, as now, wait until evening to get into full swing. It was a whole day of festivity, when, from outlying farms, lasses and lads, hired for the year, were given a day's leave and arrived early, boxom and smiling. Each cottage home was ready for them; the gleaned corn had been ground, the pie of pears had been made, from its flour, and a joint of fresh meat had been cooked.

Feast could never fall at a better time: harvest earnings were in hand, and garden and orchard everywhere were at the crown of their yield of plenty. Winter's pinch had not yet begun; autumn still smiled with benevolent cheer; it was the hour not to worry about past or future, but to enjoy the delights of the present. And this, by all accounts, they certainly did. I have heard of ploughmen not able to afford to lose the day's labour, who would rise extra early and be out on the fields when it was barely possible to see the furrows, so that they might knock off for the Feast before noon. For the thrill of anticipation was in every heart; it seemed to all to be the violation of deep-rooted sentiment, to work on the day of the Feast.

Inquiries, made of old men, revealed that the amusements were homely enough — skittles, the dancing booth, and visiting clowns. The professional up-to-date roundabouts, swings, shooting galleries, and all the rest, had not been heard of; though one villager — Master Picot — seems to have anticipated the Galloping Horses, for he made a set of his own out of elm slabs and iron bars, which he rigged up on the green each year. The motive power was supplied by boys, who pushed their more fortunate comrades round and round for the rate of a free ride now and then. Master Picot kept a stick handy for anyone else who attempted a ride on the sly. So far as I know, only one joke made by a visiting clown has come down the years. They asked him: "What was the thinnest thing he had ever seen?" and he said it was the thick end of a piece of cheese that he had bought with bread at the *Dragon* that day for twopence. And when they told him that his tale was impossible what about the thin end — he vowed that the thin end was so thin that he could not see it at all!

These were the pleasures of our fathers in those far-off days before our present excess of provided amusements had dulled the natural edge of enjoyment.

The Mummers

When the last of summer had given place to the fullness of late November, when fogs were prevalent and the darkness each evening was of a kind that made it easier to tread the village ways by their feel underfoot rather than by any attempt at sight; then, as for centuries before, on the twenty-fourth day of the month a company of youths performed the traditional fight of King George with the Turkish Knight.

They repeated those stereotyped phrases and performed every separate act of the drama as strictly as if it had been a religious duty, as their fathers had done before them; and in neither did they attempt the slightest deviation of speech or gesture. No script of the play existed; the old men of the village knew every word and act to the last letter; they had performed the play themselves when they were young, and would not have tolerated anything different, no matter how much of an improvement it may have been from a dramatic standpoint.

The Mummers' performance was undoubtedly a notable unchanged survival of very ancient rural life, coming down from a past altogether too remote for anything definite of its origin to be known. Yet the sudden flinging open of the door, and the announced entry, with the subsequent fight that needed ample space to be properly rendered, immediately suggest a far ruder order of life: the common homestead in some forest clearing, where on the dark winter evening such a visit from a neighbouring settlement would be cheerfully welcome.

In fact, a little imagination gave the play, as it was rendered in the homes of my village, an interest far beyond its actual performance. It was possible to see history in it; to see not only the play but its original setting: the common home, the blaze of its central fire made all the brighter within by the gloom of the surrounding forest. To the people in such forest settlements such boisterous plays offered perhaps the only outlet for the spirit of youth. Reading they had none; they had old tales to tell of exploits more or less true, and fables of the supernatural, on which to feed their minds, ever sensitive to the influences of both occult and real. The Yuletide spirit, too, was at work with them at such a time, or rather the far more ancient response of the human heart to the mid-winter turning of the days, with its joyous celebrations, of which the visit of the "Katterners" or "Mummers" — as they were called — was an announcement and a beginning.

Although these conditions of life had changed completely, of course, at the time of my youth it was apparent that even then the play was rendered almost in its original form. The traditional insistence upon keeping to the exact words and actions made this more certain; though King George, one suspected, had superseded an earlier St George. The allusions to beer and feasting indicated what was probably the climax to the performance in ancient times.

I well remember following the players down the village street: *Number One*, the first player, with besom in hand, flinging open the house doors in succession and entering with the bold announcement:

"A room! A room! Brave gallants, room!
I come to show you merry sports and sights
upon this dark and wintry night.
New activity; old activity:
such activity as never was seen before

and perhaps will never be seen no more.
Come in, my next head man."

Thereupon entered *Old Father Christmas*, bent with age and with beard hoary from the passage of years. Thumping his gnarled stick heavily on the floor, he said:

"In comes I, Old Father Christmas!
Welcome or welcome not.
I hope Old Father Christmas will never be forgot.
For in this room there shall be shown
The dreadfulest battle that ever was known."

Number One, standing aside, then sharply re-announced:

"Come in, my next head man."

Then entered *King George*, regally dressed and with sword in hand, saying:

"In comes I, King George, King George,
The man of courage bold.
With this, my broad sword, in my hand,
I won ten pounds in gold.
I fought the fiery dragon
And drove him to the slaughter.
And by the means of that I won
The King of Egypt's daughter.
Let e'er a man defy me, I'll hack him to the finest dust and send him to college to make mince pie crust."

Number One:

"Come in, my next head man."

Then would enter the *Turkish Knight*, in fighting garb resplendent, and deportment braggart. Swinging his sword he made his fearless declaration:

"In comes I, the Turkish Knight.
From Turkey's land I've come to fight.
Fight thee, King George, thou man of courage bold.
And if thy blood be hot, I'll quickly fetch it cold."

To which *King George*, with superior and dignified mien, replied:

"What-ho, thou merry fellow! Thou talkest very
  bold;
just like the young Turks as I've been told.
Therefore, thou Turkish Knight,
pull out thy sword and fight.
pull out thy purse and pay;
for I mean to have satisfaction
before thou goest away."

Turkish Knight replying, undaunted and unashamed:

"Satisfaction? No satisfaction at all!
My head is made of iron and my body is lined
  with steel,

and I will battle with thee, King George,
to see which of us on the ground this day shall lie.
So guard your head and guard your nose
and guard your body, and down you goes."

Fencing commenced before this brave speech ended.
King George, receiving a nasty thrust from the sword of
the *Turkish Knight*, fell, one knee to the ground. *Turkish
Knight* stood aside. *King George* made effort, and
slowly rising, said:

"No! Think I've done with thee, Turkish Knight?
I will arise and show thee my might.
So guard your head and guard your nose
and guard your body, and down you goes."

A sharper conflict followed, in which *Turkish Knight*
received a deadly thrust from the sword of *King George*,
and straightway fell groaning to the earth. Then *Father
Christmas*, running forward, held his arms over the
prostrate body, saying:

"Is there a doctor to be found,
that can raise this poor man that lies bleeding on
  the ground?"

Whereupon the *Doctor* appeared, dressed (in my days)
in frock coat and top hat, and saying with a dignity that
arises from sure knowledge:

"Yes! There is a doctor to be found
that can raise this man that lies bleeding on
   the ground."

Father Christmas:

"Doctor, what is thy fee?"

Doctor:

"Ten guineas is my fee;
but ten pounds I'll take of thee."

Father Christmas:

"Doctor, what canst thou cure?"

Doctor:

"I can cure the hip, the pip,
the palsy, or the gout;
the roaming pains within or out:
the gaping pains and the measles.
Bring me an old woman, threescore years and ten,
without a single tooth in her head; I'll set her up,
   young and plump again.
For I carry a bottle by my side
called "Old Ecclestone Pain".
One drop on this man's brow
and another on his tongue,
will strike through this man's body
and raise him from the ground again."

203

And the *Doctor* applied his cure without waiting, which instantly had the ascribed effect. Then *King George*, seeing the result, thus addressed the *Turkish Knight*:

"Rise! Rise! thou cowardly dog,
and go home to shine own country
and tell them what Old England has done for thee.
And tell them that we'll fight
ten thousand better men than thee!"

Turkish Knight thereupon arose from the earth and retired, *Number One* announcing,

"Come in, my next head man."

Then appeared *Johnny Jack*, a diminutive youth carrying a large youth on his back. Staggering along under his burden, he perkily announced:

"In comes I, Old Johnny Jack,
with my wife and family on my back!
My family is large, though I am small,
and a little money would help us all.
Roast beef, plum puddings, mince pies, jam tarts;
who likes them better than Old Father Christmas
  and I?
For one mug of your Christmas ale
would make us all merry and sing;
and money in our pockets is
a very fine thing.

So ladies and gentlemen, sit at your ease
and find us what money you can, if you please."

Johnny Jack, handing his hat to the assembled company, collected their contributions, after which the players — often refreshed as well with ale or home-made wines — united in local song and dance, before dispersing to do the whole mummery over again at the next place of call.

Towards the end of the nineteenth century, zeal for conventions exceeded the ardour of the village to maintain this truly historic play. The police made it their duty to hover on the heels of the players, keeping a watch on their conduct; so that they became fearful of making unannounced entry to a private house. Thus it was, that, in the last years of the Mummers, the public-house became almost the only place where the play could be rendered correctly.

Thomassing

On the twenty-first of December each year the old dames of the village, going about in pairs, canvassed those who could afford it for alms. Their attitude was not one of indigent poverty; they came in recognition of a time-honoured custom, a rite that needed no other explanation but the plain announcement, "If you please, we've come a-thomassing". As a custom it was interesting and picturesque, but it was certainly evidence of an earlier poverty, and we may be glad that the granting of old age pensions brought it to an end. Yet one old lady (to her honour) still keeps the custom going — to whom, if it be my last, my sixpence shall be given.

Mayday

Of all the yearly celebrations Mayday lasted the latest in continuous observance. None was more truly beautiful in its expression, or more historic.

A cynic might say that it was no more than a crowd of children with garlands of flowers badgering the houses for coppers, a nuisance to neighbours and demoralizing for the children; but properly seen, Mayday was a genuine survival of an old and genuine sentiment, an expression of the joy felt at the coming of spring again, the response of country spirits to the renewal of warmth and sunshine and the return of the beauty of leaf and flower spread over the land.

No explanation tells us why, when the custom had ceased in so many parts, it should have held on in our village and the neighbourhood; perhaps the explanation didn't matter very much. It was enough to know that Mayday reached back far beyond record; that it was the contemporary expression of a very constant and ancient influence: the impelling spell of beauty, that has ever held the soul of mankind within its purifying power. It gave a happy occasion, too, for the expression of kindness. In one neighbouring village sixpence was given at the door of the manor house to every child that called on Mayday. And one boy, who at a tender age had started work to lead the plough team, begged leave of absence and ran there and back rather than lose so cherished a gift.

The children went round, either singly with a simple garland on a stick, or in twos with an interwoven festoon. They did not understand its ancient significance; to them it was a grand day of freedom from school, a day, by custom and unwritten law, particularly their own. They sang their simple songs wishing each household a happy day, they collected their pennies and carried them off to certain cottages, where on that day only each year, sweets called *Suckballs* were made and sold.

The compound from which those *Suckballs* were made was boiled and poured out on to sheets of newspaper, each sweet forming a disc the size and shape of a small round biscuit. When they had hardened, the whole paper of them was displayed in the lattice windows of the cottages. The children bought them (about six for a penny) still on their newspaper, the cottage wife cutting them off with scissors as she sold them.

But this absence from school seems not to have suited the convenience of the teachers; and historic interest was of small account beside that claim. Sentiment, too, went for nothing in the heads of the prudish, who argued that children should not be encouraged to get something for nothing, and by and by curt officialdom disallowed the holiday and, in consequence, the Mayday celebration is almost disregarded.

CHAPTER
SIXTEEN

The Skeleton
in the Cupboard

Lest anyone be tempted by these memories of boyhood to conclude that village life was a continuous flow of happy melody, it is right in the interests of truth to record the dismal ogre that haunted the lives of scores of young villagers with perpetual menace.

Some called it "consumption", others "decline", a dread complaint that claimed its victims so relentlessly that the village at that time was never free from it. The symptoms were always the same: a delicate flush on an otherwise pale face, accompanied by a short, hacking cough; this continued for about three years, the sick one becoming weaker, until the end. There was no time of my early life when this experience was not daily before my eyes, the afflicted ones often being relatives or friends.

It was only too easy to note that their dispositions resembled one's own, and that they had weaknesses to be found also in oneself. This thought, brooded on, became a perpetual secret fear, and the secret was strengthened by chance remarks of certain folk who seemed to take a morbid pleasure in naming those for whom they foresaw or feared a similar fate. They would ask anxiously about someone's health, and say with a sigh how strong was the resemblance to the one lately taken away. These simple factors, that now seem absurd to write, were then potent with fear that spoiled the joy of scores of young lives and may have lessened the powers of resistance.

Had I not believed myself to have been one so unhappily chosen I could not have understood the feeling as I did; yet with the belief a feeling of resentment came, a determination not to go under without a struggle. A chance reading about breathing exercises as a precaution led me to adopt it daily. Every night, unknown to anyone, I bared my chest and filled my lungs slowly through the nose, and, after holding the wind for a few moments, allowed it to escape through the mouth. This I continued throughout the years from boyhood to manhood, not telling anyone, or knowing whether it did me good or ill.

Life was sweet and my mind ever sensitive to its alluring beauty. To know it to the full in the fellowship and love of friends, and to experience the joys of a healthy life, was my ambition. Yet the fear persisted; there was no mistaking the fact that I had the same disposition, temperament, and frailties of flesh as near relatives who had fallen before the common foe. I cast about for expedients and, being on my own resources, away from home, purchased fresh eggs and sucked them raw, and even adopted a local remedy, which my father often said had saved the life of one man he knew — the

209

eating of live garden snails.

Only the determination to hold on to young sweet life at all costs could have enabled me to overcome the first repugnance; to have taken a big snail by the shell and to have withdrawn it by the teeth and masticated it! Yet, to my surprise, it was wonderfully sweet and delicious in flavour; as indeed should reasonably be expected in a creature that feeds only on pure vegetables; moreover, snails seemed to have a nutritive value equal to that of the oyster. Other local remedies of the same kind belonged to old-time rural life. I recall a native who swallowed one live frog each spring, which, he held, maintained his health through the summer.

In spite of much that was beautiful in times now gone for ever, the single fact that medical science has mastered so many dread diseases in my own lifetime makes me realize once again at what a fortunate time I was born. My father often told us that we had no idea of the perpetual dread of smallpox at the time of his youth, when it was usual to see one out of every three faces pitted with the scars. Many factors of modern life have helped to overcome these terrors of past days, not least as I believe, the many good varieties of food now to be bought; and, of course, the vast improvement of sanitation, and the greater comforts of home life.

The rough life of our fathers was suitable only to the strong in constitution; the weaklings went under.

SCOTTISH
BORDERS
LIBRARY
SERVICE